Students Must Write

A guide to better writing in coursework and examinations

Third edition

Robert Barrass

Routledge
Taylor & Francis Group

LONDON AND NEW YORK

First published 1982 by Methuen & Co. Ltd
Second edition published 1995 by Routledge
Third edition published 2005 by Routledge
2 Park Square, Milton Park, Abingdon, Oxon OX14 4RN

Simultaneously published in the USA and Canada by Routledge
270 Madison Ave, New York, NY 10016

Reprinted 2007

Routledge is an imprint of the Taylor & Francis Group, an informa business

Typeset in Goudy by The Running Head Limited, Cambridge
Printed and bound in Great Britain by MPG Books Ltd, Bodmin

British Library Cataloguing in Publication Data
A catalogue record for this book is available from the British Library

Library of Congress Cataloging in Publication Data
A catalog record for this book has been requested

ISBN 10: 0–415–35826–4 (Pbk)
ISBN 10: 0–415–35825–6 (Hbk)
ISBN 13: 978–0–415–35826–2 (Pbk)
ISBN 13: 978–0–415–35825–5 (Hbk)

Contents

Figures and tables

Figures

Tables

Preface

The ability to express yourself is an essential basis for success as a student, when applying for employment and in any career. In all academic subjects students must write, and all teachers and lecturers should encourage their students to write well. This book, therefore, is for all students: both (a) for those who know that their written work does not give a true indication of their ability, who accept that if they could improve their writing they could score higher marks in all coursework and examinations, and (b) for those who although satisfied that they write well are prepared to consider the possibility of improvement. By improving their writing all students should be able to improve the quality of their thinking – because writing and thinking are very closely associated – and by submitting better written work for assessment they should achieve higher grades.

In this third edition account is taken of the increasing use of computers over the past ten years, for information retrieval and in preparing written assignments as part of coursework. The order of presentation reflects the changing needs of students from the first to the final year of a degree or diploma course. I hope it will help all students, whether they are continuing their education soon after leaving school, studying part-time while in employment, or returning to college or university after a period in full-time employment. Changes have been made in all chapters, and some have been completely revised, but my purpose has not changed: this is to provide a guide to better writing that students can read, perhaps one chapter each week when they start a college or university course, and then keep to hand for reference whenever they need help with their writing.

Most chapters end with a section headed *Improve your writing* which includes exercises that may be undertaken by students working alone or used by tutors as ideas for use in their courses on written communication.

Robert Barrass

Acknowledgements

This book is based on my experience as a principal lecturer at the University of Sunderland. I write not as a grammarian but as a teacher, tutor and administrator. My intention is to help students of all subjects to think clearly and to express their thoughts effectively in writing.

For their help in preparing this third edition, I thank Jonathan Barrass who advised on the use of computers as an aid to planning and writing; Jane Moore of the University of Sunderland's Murray Library who read the typescript for the chapter on finding and using information; both Margaret Parsons of the School of Education and Lifelong Learning and Robert Jewitt of the School of Languages, Communications and Culture who read the whole typescript; and both Trevor Hartley and Norman Catcherside of the School of Health, Natural and Social Sciences who gave IT support and advice. I also thank Adrian Burrows who drew the cartoons; and Ann, my wife, for her interest, encouragement and help in preparing successive editions.

The comments on the writing of 18-year-old students in the UK, included in chapters 1 and 10, are based on examiners' reports. But the examples of poor English included in chapters 3 and 6, with suggested improvements, are all from books – some from books on writing – not from the written work of students. Like Gowers (1986), I do not give the source of such extracts.

1 Judged by your writing

If your long-term objective in study is to achieve your full potential, and obtain the highest grades of which you are capable, consider three reasons why many students underachieve.

1   Some lack motivation, and do not work hard enough.
2   Many attend classes and work hard, but have poor time management skills and do not study effectively.
3   More do study effectively and know their work, yet underachieve because they pay insufficient attention to improving their ability to communicate their thoughts in writing.

Effective writing as the basis for success

Writing is important in studying all subjects, and in all professions. Only by writing well can you give a good account of yourself as a student or when applying for employment, or in a career when writing e-mails, memoranda, letters, instructions and reports. It is by your writing that many people judge you (see Table 1.1).

If you are to achieve your full potential as a student, and progress in your chosen career, the ability to express yourself clearly, concisely and persuasively in writing is an essential skill that you should be trying to develop.

As a student you write with a pen for several hours each day, making notes in lectures, practical classes, seminars, tutorials and private study. And you write using a word processor when completing important coursework assignments, project reports and theses. You score marks for all your written work, both indirectly if you make good notes when studying and directly if you communicate your thoughts effectively in assessed coursework, tests and examinations.

Table 1.1 Judged by your writing

Characteristics of your writing	Impression created
(a) Desirable	*Favourable*
Clearly expressed	Clear thinking
Spelling correct	Well educated
Punctuation and grammar good	Competent
Well presented	Well organised
Helpful	Considerate
(b) Undesirable	*Unfavourable*
Badly expressed	Inconsiderate
Spelling poor	Lazy
Punctuation and grammar poor	Careless
Badly presented	Incompetent
Handwriting illegible	Inconsiderate

It is mainly by the quality of your writing that assessors find out what you know and how much you understand, and judge the quality of your thinking. In any assessed written work, if two students were otherwise equal in ability and intelligence you would expect the one who was the better able to convey thoughts effectively in writing to score the higher marks. So it is important to recognise, from the start of your course, that your final grades will depend not only on your knowledge and understanding of your subject but also on how well you are able to convey this knowledge and understanding in writing.

All learning depends on the understanding and effective use of language; and the purpose of all education should be to help students develop the ability to think critically, and to express their thoughts effectively whether speaking or writing. They should also be encouraged to read critically – thinking about what they read – because reading, supported by observation and conversation, is the key to knowledge. There is nothing new in these assertions.

For example, the report of a government committee of inquiry into the teaching of English in England (Newbolt, 1921) emphasised: (a) that all children must be taught to speak well before they can learn to write well; (b) that English, as the instrument of thought for English-speaking people, provides the basis for teaching all subjects; (c) that every teacher, teaching in English, is a teacher of English [because we learn by example, as well as by specific instruction]; (d) that education should be 'guidance in the acquiring of experience'; and (e) that the appreciation of English literature is important not only for the pleasure to be derived from reading but also as 'the lasting communication of experience' and as a good influence on the reader's own use of the language.

These thoughts were summarised by George Sampson, a member of the Newbolt committee, and 25 years later by Dorothy L. Sayers and by Eric Partridge.

English . . . includes and transcends all subjects. It is for English people the whole means of expression, the attainment of which makes them articulate and intelligible human beings, able to inherit the past, to possess the present and to confront the future. It is English in this sense that we must teach our children all day long, at all stages of their school life.

. . . every teacher is a teacher of English because every teacher is a teacher in English.

English for the English, George Sampson (1925)

Modern education concentrates on teaching subjects, leaving the method of thinking, arguing and expressing one's conclusions to be picked up by the [scholars as they go along . . . Teachers] are doing for their pupils the work which the pupils themselves ought to do. For the sole true end of education is simply this: to teach [people] how to learn for themselves; and whatever instruction fails to do this is effort spent in vain.

The Lost Tools of Learning, Dorothy L. Sayers (1948)

If only teachers [of all subjects] would teach their pupils to think out every problem, and insist that all questions be answered thoughtfully and clearly, this salutary and indeed indispensable discipline and exercise of the mind would immensely improve the pupil's speech and writing, not merely in the English class but also in every other, both at school and outside.

English: A Course for Human Beings, Eric Partridge (1949)

A further 25 years later the need to teach English Language across the curriculum was also the main point made in the report of another government inquiry into the teaching of English (Bullock, 1975); and its relevance to the study of all academic subjects was further emphasised in the 1980s in examiners' reports on the written work of 18-year-old students.

English language and literature

Some students wrote with charm and intelligence, displaying a love of books and of scholarship. Their work, written in clear, direct and simple English, was a delight to read. Others with limited practice in essay, précis, summary and comprehension techniques were easily identified. And there were also candidates who displayed in their writing a contempt for our language.

Most candidates should spend more time thinking about the meaning of the question and the words used, and should plan their work. They would then be able to write a considered answer. With such thought, the standard of answers would be raised.

English law

Many candidates took no notice of the actual question set. Instead they wrote *all that they knew* about the subject and thus not only wasted valuable time but also demonstrated that they did not have a proper understanding of the subject.

Too many candidates fail to appreciate that a lawyer cannot function without a command of accurate punctuation and grammar. Bad English means bad law.

Engineering science

Particular attention is drawn to the deplorable English of some candidates . . . poor sentence construction . . . lack of lucidity . . . dreadful spelling. This is a pity because in both higher education and industry great importance is attached to comprehension and communication skills.

History

The best scripts revealed an excellent knowledge and understanding of the topic discussed; and an ability to write an organized, fluent and cogent answer.

Time spent on teaching the art of writing is not time wasted. Even weaker candidates obtain higher marks after they have been properly taught to plan their answers and then to write concisely, intelligibly and in an orderly manner.

Everyone is capable of self-improvement. Good candidates can do better. Inevitably, clever candidates do not do as well as they should if they have not been properly trained in examination techniques.

Geography

The best candidates showed skill and perception when interpreting questions and writing appropriate answers. But some students with a great fund of knowledge do not achieve their full potential because they are unable to make intelligent use of their material. If they are to score high marks, students must learn how to answer the different types of questions they encounter in examinations and they must acquire sound skills in composition and in basic examination techniques.

Unfortunately, there are many candidates who fail to benefit from their knowledge of geography because mistakes in grammar and spelling render them incapable of expressing themselves unambiguously.

Even the most able 18-year-olds, who sit scholarship examinations, do not write as well as they should. Consider, for example, the following comments from an examiner's report on a scholarship paper in biology.

All answers included much irrelevant information.
Looseness of expression indicated lack of careful thought.
Very few answers were comprehensive.
Even when they knew the answer many candidates had difficulty in bringing facts together in an effective order.
Many candidates had the knowledge but were unable to express themselves.

The best English is to be expected from students of English literature but, in their report on a paper on critical appreciation, examiners noted that standards of punctuation and spelling, as well of grammar, are declining. 'Even quite good candidates spell words as though they have never seen them before, varying their spelling from one occasion to the next. This decline in literacy, now *very* marked, should be a matter of great concern.'

Examiners' findings that even clever school-leavers have difficulty with spelling, punctuation and grammar, and in selecting, arranging and expressing their thoughts, are one source of concern about the way English is taught in schools. Another is the complaints of employers about the poor communication skills of students leaving schools, colleges and universities, who in their places of work write e-mails, letters, memoranda, instructions and reports expressed in English that is incomprehensible, or in which the misuse of words and of emphasis result in misunderstandings, costly mistakes and accidents.

Yet another government report on the teaching of English Language in British schools (Kingman, 1988) addressed these concerns and, like the earlier reports (Newbolt, 1921 and Bullock, 1975), recommended changes in teacher training and in English teaching, in an attempt to ensure: (a) that *all teachers* have *some explicit knowledge* of the facts and uses of the English language *and are able to help* their pupils to develop the ability to write clearly and accurately in standard English, and (b) that their pupils are familiar with such terms as pronoun, verb, sentence, full stop, comma and paragraph, can understand their meaning, and can use this understanding both when they or their teachers talk about the language and when they need to recognise and correct faults in their own work (Kingman, 1988).

Whereas in the 1920s employers were complaining about deficiencies in use of English by 14-year-old school-leavers (Newbolt, 1921), in the 1970s and 1990s they were complaining of the poor English of 16- to 18-year-old school-leavers (Bullock, 1975; Kingman, 1988), and of those aged 21, or more, leaving colleges and universities (Dearing, 1997; Mullen, 1997). Dearing found 'no consensus among employers as to the main deficiencies [in key skills] of people entering employment, from higher education', but about a quarter complained of inadequate communication skills.

Regrettably, after more than 12 years at school, many students starting courses in higher education are clever enough to understand their work and yet unable to communicate their knowledge, understanding and ideas effectively. They need help in developing their communications skills (Wojtas, 1981). Many need help with their writing more than they need further instruction in their chosen subjects.

So teachers of all subjects, in further and higher education as well as in schools, should play their part in helping their students improve their use of words. Students are unlikely to appreciate how important writing is, in studying their subjects, and in any career based on their studies, if it is only the teachers of English at school and the tutors responsible for courses in communication skills in further and higher education establishments who encourage them to improve their use of English.

Could you improve your writing?

In view of the importance of writing in studying all subjects, and when applying for employment, and afterwards whenever they need to express their thoughts clearly and persuasively in writing, all students should be intent on improving their written work.

Those who are unable to express themselves clearly when they leave school do not suddenly acquire this ability, without effort, when they go on to college or university. If they are to improve their basic writing skills they will have to practise writing themselves, and will continue to need encouragement, constructive criticism and advice.

What is perhaps not so obvious is that those students who write well should also be trying, with encouragement and advice, to improve their writing and so to score even higher marks in their assessed coursework and in examinations.

All teachers in schools and in higher education should help all their students to develop the ability to think – and to express thoughts clearly and convincingly – so that their writing is interesting, persuasive, and a pleasure to read.

Some key skills

All students need to develop certain skills which, because they provide a basis for success in studying any subject, are called core skills or study skills. Because they are needed for success in all professions, as well as in studying all subjects, these personal skills are also called common skills, enterprise skills, key skills or transferable skills (see Table 1.2).

Your style of writing reflects your whole personality, and improving your ability to express yourself clearly and convincingly in speaking and writing is part of your continuing personal development. Therefore, before considering why students must write (chapter 2) and how students should write (chapter 3), consider three other life skills needed as a basis for effective study and for success in any career: self management, money management and time management.

Self management

Think of study as employment. Ask yourself why you are devoting several years of your life (if you are studying full-time) or so much of what might otherwise be devoted to leisure activities (if you are studying part-time) to your studies. What would you like to achieve?

To give direction to your studies, it is a good idea to list your long-term objectives (for example, to progress on your course of study and achieve grades that are a true reflection of your ability, and to progress in a particular career). Then decide how you will organise other aspects of your life, not just your studies, to help you achieve these objectives.

Table 1.2 Some skills needed in studying any subject and in any profession

Personal skills	Why some students under-achieve
1 Self management	Not working hard enough or effort poorly directed. Overwork. Personal problems. Problems with relationships.
2 Money management	Worries about money.
3 Time management	Lack of planning: ineffective use of time for study, recreation and rest.
4 Summarising	Inability to distinguish important points from the supporting detail. Not making good notes in organised classes and in private study.
5 Finding information	Not making good use of libraries and other sources of ideas and information.
6 Processing information	Not bringing together relevant information and ideas from lectures, tutorials, seminars, practical work, background reading and other sources.
7 Problem solving	Not thinking things through to a satisfactory conclusion.
8 Thinking and creativity	Mindless repetition of other people's thoughts: unwillingness to consider new approaches or different points of view.
9 Communicating	Not expressing thoughts clearly, concisely and convincingly when speaking and writing.

1 As the essential basis for good health, so that you keep fit for study and can enjoy life, ensure that you have a balanced diet, with enough but not too much to eat and drink each day.

2 Take exercise, appropriate to your age, both to provide a change from studying and to help you concentrate when you resume your studies. When you walk or swim, for example, the muscles of your arms and legs contract repeatedly, you breathe more frequently and more deeply than when you are inactive, and your heart beats faster – increasing the flow of blood through all parts of your body. This is why, after exercise, you are alert, have a feeling of well-being, and are refreshed.

3 Ensure that you have enough sleep, so that you wake feeling refreshed and are always alert when you need to concentrate. Most adults need about eight hours' sleep each night – and if they go late to bed are not at their best mentally or physically on the next day.

Money management

Financial planning is important, from the start of a full-time course, so that you can try to live within your means. If as a full-time student you also work part-time to increase your income, this will leave you less time for other things that should be part of student life or for private study – and so may make it more difficult for you to achieve your long-term objectives. Financial planning is also important for a part-time student, even with an income from full-time paid employment, because extra expenses are likely to result from course fees, and from the cost of travel, books and equipment that might not otherwise have been necessary.

Time management

Organising your studies, to promote effective learning and to avoid stress, is largely a matter of allocating your time and then concentrating on essentials.

As a student some of the time you devote to study is organised for you, as indicated in your timetable, but you must accept responsibility for your own learning. From the start of any course you need to organise the rest of your time – each week – to ensure that you devote enough time to study and enough to recreation, and that hours are not lost in procrastination. For example, look at your timetable to see when there are periods that you can use for working in the library. Most people work best in the mornings, so if you are studying full-time try to make an early start each day – whether or not you have organised classes.

At the start of your course, to help you achieve your long-term objectives, set yourself medium-term objectives by listing things you plan to achieve in each year of your course, in each term or semester, before your next vacation, and in each vacation. Decide how many hours you will devote to study each week, in the evenings and at weekends: and decide when you will take time off in each vacation.

In three hours set aside for study, some students find they make more progress if they work for about an hour on each of three tasks, with a short break between tasks, rather than for three hours at one task. However, it is not possible to make rigid rules about such things – to suit everyone or every occasion.

Set yourself short-term objectives. At the end of your last study period each day, list the things you plan to do on the next day, apart from attending organised classes. For example, you may need to read a chapter in a textbook, consult a reference book in a library, seek information from other sources or ask your tutor a question. Some of the things you have to do (some tasks) cannot be done effectively in one study session, so you will need to recognise smaller tasks within these tasks – some of which can be done, or must be done, before you do the others.

In your list of tasks, distinguish those that are urgent and important (see

1	IMPORTANT URGENT Do first	2	IMPORTANT LESS URGENT Do second
3	LESS IMPORTANT URGENT Do third (today, if necessary)	4	LESS IMPORTANT LESS URGENT Need not do today

Figure 1.1   A guide to prioritising tasks, but always use your judgement and
remember that less important does not mean unimportant

Figure 1.1) from those that should come lower in order of priority. Then:
(a) number the tasks in your order of priority, (b) tick tasks off your list as
you complete them, and (c) reconsider your priorities when adding new
tasks to the list during the day or planning your next day's work.

2   Four reasons for writing

So much of what you write is intended for other people, enabling you to influence their thoughts and actions, that it is easy to overlook your other reasons for writing. You write as part of your day-to-day work: to help you to remember, to observe, and to think, as well as to communicate.

Writing helps you to remember

You probably first used writing as an aid to remembering in your early years at school when copying complete sentences – from a book or dictated by a teacher. Later, you made notes in class while a teacher was speaking, while you were reading, and during your own investigations.

Making good notes

At college or university you make more effective use of your time in each lecture, seminar or tutorial if you have made some preparations. You should therefore look at the syllabus for the examination you will be taking or at the learning objectives for your course, and at your course guide, so that you understand what is included in each part of the course; but remember that such documents are only guides. To find out exactly what your course comprises you must attend all the lectures and all other organised classes.

At the start of each part of the course, your lecturer should provide a list of the subjects to be considered each week in lectures, seminars and other organised classes; full bibliographic details of textbooks or other essential reading for this part of the course; and details of other learning resources recommended for private study. Without this information students cannot prepare for their next class, or view each class in the context of the course as a whole.

Students may also be provided with a list of learning outcomes (things that they will be expected to know, understand or be able to do by the end of the course). They should also be told how their performance will be assessed, and should be able to purchase – or to study in the library in their own time – specimen test papers similar to those they will take themselves, and copies of the examination papers actually taken by students in at least the past two years of the course.

Each lecture should begin with a concise title or a clear statement of the subject to be considered. You are advised to note the title, the lecturer's name and the date. Then listen carefully, think, and try to understand. In speech more words are used than are needed in writing, so you should not need to write all the time. Lecturers are likely to say something, and then rephrase what they have just said in an attempt to ensure that everyone understands. Then they may repeat things for emphasis; or summarise what they have said at the end of each part of their lecture to help you recognise and record the most important points. In taking notes, therefore, it is neither necessary nor desirable to record the lecturer's every word.

Take your cue from the lecturer. Sometimes, knowing that the information is not readily available from other sources, the lecturer may repeat important points for emphasis – almost as in a dictation. At other times the lecturer will speak quickly, and you will be able to write only carefully selected headings for each new subject discussed, and sub-headings for each aspect of the subject (that is to say, for each topic).

Note the main points as key words and phrases. Use abbreviations. Record numbers, names, dates and titles. Write definitions carefully, as they are dictated. Record the lecturer's conclusions clearly and concisely.

Mark any points that you do not understand, perhaps by a question mark in the left-hand margin. Then you will be ready to ask questions at the end. Note the answers to your questions, and anything in the answers to other students' questions that contributes to your understanding.

Copy simple diagrams carefully while the lecturer is drawing on a flipchart or board; and you should be allowed time to study any diagram or table, projected on a screen or displayed as a map or chart, in silence, before the lecturer offers further explanation or moves on to the next topic.

Most lecturers write on a board or project images on to a screen: (a) to display the title of their lecture, (b) to provide main headings, (c) to emphasise certain aspects, and (d) to summarise essential points at the end. If the lecture has been well planned, your notes should contain a summary of the main points. These may be arranged as an orderly sequence of topic words and phrases, as numbered headings, with some supporting detail, similar to the outline prepared by the lecturer when deciding what to say.

However, such sequential notes that preserve the order in which a lecturer presents information – or develops ideas – are more appropriate in some subjects than in others. There is no one correct way to make notes.

Table 2.1 Making good notes as an aid to thinking and learning

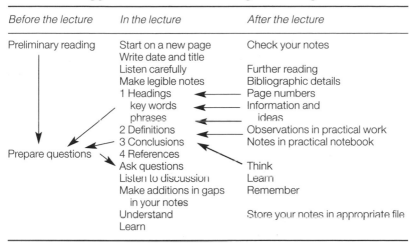

Before the lecture	In the lecture	After the lecture
Preliminary reading	Start on a new page	Check your notes
	Write date and title	
	Listen carefully	Further reading
	Make legible notes	Bibliographic details
	1 Headings	Page numbers
	key words	Information and
	phrases	ideas
	2 Definitions	Observations in practical work
	3 Conclusions	Notes in practical notebook
Prepare questions	4 References	
	Ask questions	Think
	Listen to discussion	Learn
	Make additions in gaps	Remember
	in your notes	
	Understand	Store your notes in appropriate file
	Learn	

Note
The preliminary reading will help you to understand the lecture better than would otherwise be possible, and to make better notes, as well as to prepare questions. The arrows in this table represent additions to your notes as a result of work done before and after the lecture.

You may prefer to arrange them in some other way, which you find helps you to listen and to learn.

At first as a student you may take too many notes, but with experience you are likely to become more selective – and as you develop your notemaking skills you are likely to prepare different kinds of notes on different occasions, depending on the way a lecture or seminar is organised, and on your purpose.

Remember that the lecturer's task is not to provide you with a neat set of notes – by dictating a summary of your textbook – but to provide a digest of the essentials of the subject supported by examples; to discuss problems, hypotheses and evidence; to explain difficult points, concepts and principles; to refer to sources of further information; and to answer questions. In this way the lecturer acts as a guide and pacemaker. By listening, thinking and understanding, you are able to move forward more quickly than would be possible if you worked alone. However, you will find it easier to understand and to make useful notes during a lecture if you have done some preliminary reading (see Table 2.1) and if you have understood the earlier lectures in the same course.

You should either listen to the lecture and then go to your books, and to other sources of information, or make notes as you follow the lecturer's explanations, arguments and conclusions. Whichever method you adopt, you need to concentrate on what is being said so that you learn throughout each lecture and are ready to ask or to answer questions at the end. Making notes helps you to remain attentive (see Figure 2.1); and in selecting the most important points to record you distinguish what is most important from the supporting explanation and the details. See also *Make good notes as you read*, page 127.

Good concise notes help you to remember the essentials of a subject. They can be read and re-read, and you can add to them throughout your course of study as you get a firmer grasp of your subject. Concise notes are an aid to all your studies and they are essential when you are revising for examinations and do not have time to read copious detailed notes.

Use a pad of loose-leaf wide-lined A4 paper (210 × 297 mm) for all your written work. Narrow-lined paper is unsuitable for either your own notes or handwritten assignments because there is no space between the lines for minor additions or corrections. In making notes leave wide margins and leave gaps where you expect to make additions. You are also advised to write on only one side of each sheet – so that you can insert extra sheets of notes, based on your own observations in practical work, on your reading, and on your own thoughts about the subject, in appropriate files. Your aim should be to have one set of notes (one file) on each aspect of your work (see Figure 9.2).

Making notes is an aid to concentration, to active study, and to learning. Because they are so important, try to make good notes from the start of your course. A bound notebook may be best for some purposes: for example, for a laboratory or field notebook in which it is essential to keep records in chronological order with a note of the date at the start of each day's work and of the time when each note is made. Otherwise there are advantages in using loose-leaf paper.

1   Notes on any topic can be kept together.
2   Pages can be added or removed easily.
3   The order of topics can be changed.
4   All your work on a subject (for example, your notes and assessed course-work) can be kept in one file (see page 131).
5   It is normally necessary to carry only notepaper and writing materials. Notes made in different lectures or in the library can then be transferred to the appropriate subject file quickly, each evening.
6   You will be less likely to lose all your notes on any subject – the result of one, two or three years' work – than you would be if you were to take them with you to the library, to lectures and to other classes.

Note-taking helps you remain attentive

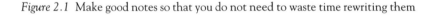

Figure 2.1 Make good notes so that you do not need to waste time rewriting them

Try to develop your note-taking skills so that you can make concise notes as you participate in all your lectures, seminars and tutorials. Then check your notes, as soon as possible after each class, while the ideas and information are fresh in your mind. Check that they are legible and that you can understand them. Make corrections and minor additions.

Some students carry a bound notebook in which they make all their class notes, and then spend time each evening copying notes on different subjects into appropriate files kept at home. However, you are advised not to get into the habit of copying out notes. This is likely to be a waste of time; and in copying you may make mistakes. Furthermore, if you spend much time making notes in organised classes you will not have other time to spare for copying out all your class notes. Your study time is best spent on regular study, and on improving your notes (see page 130) as you learn more about your subjects.

Writing helps you to observe

Preparing an accurate description, of things observed using your five senses, helps you to concentrate your attention on an object or event, as you must when recording things you can see in an accurate line drawing (see Figure 7.1). When you have covered one point adequately in a description, look for something else to describe. This will help you to ensure that your description is complete.

Observation is clearly more important in some subjects than in others, but it is important in the arts and humanities as well as in the sciences and engineering. For example, observation is the basis of journalism – the reporting of current events – and of history – the interpretation of records of past events. Similarly, observation is more important in some careers than in others.

However, a carefully prepared description of an object or event may be part of any investigation, as a student or in other employment. As appropriate, your writing – the whole or part of any composition – may be *descriptive* (a description of people, objects, scenes, etc.) or it may be *narrative* (a description of an event or sequence of events in chronological order).

The vividness of imaginative writing depends on accuracy and clarity, and its expressiveness on the choice and use of words; and in narration the right atmosphere has been created if the reader feels part of the scene, or as if witnessing the event described.

Making notes in practical work

As in a lecture, whether you are indoors or engaged in field studies, write first the date and then a concise title that makes your purpose clear. Then record what you do and how you do it. Your notes are for your own use, so you must ensure that you will be able to understand them later and, if necessary, write a report on the work – including enough details of your materials and methods for someone with appropriate knowledge and experience to understand your report, undertake a similar investigation and record similar data.

If possible, record your observations on data sheets prepared in advance. Data sheets are tables in which the first column (the stub) may have the heading *Date and time* and each of the other columns has a heading to indicate what was observed or measured each time entries were made, and the units of measurement (see Table 7.1).

Before an investigation, preparing a data sheet helps you, as you plan the work, to decide what is to be observed and in what order the observations are to be recorded.

During the investigation a data sheet reminds you when measurements have to be made, and helps you ensure that a complete record is kept.

After the investigation, because your data are neatly arranged, the data sheet facilitates data processing to derive results that may be included in your report of the work.

In practical work, notes must not be made in rough and copied out neatly later. This would not only be a waste of time but also, and more important, you could make mistakes in copying. Instead, legible and carefully worded sentences should be written when each observation is made, supplemented where appropriate by diagrams, by annotated drawings (see Figure 7.1), or by numbers recorded on data sheets.

Your practical notebook, like a diary, serves as your permanent record of what you did each day (see page 14); but it is also the basis for any report of the work that you may need to prepare for other people.

Writing helps you to think

Capturing your thoughts

Get into the habit of making a note of useful thoughts as they come to mind. Keep a few sheets of notepaper folded in your pocket so that you can note, for example, points to be included in a composition you are planning, an idea for an interesting first paragraph, or the wording for a striking conclusion. Without such notes, your fleeting thoughts may be lost.

In *Goodbye to All That* (1957) Robert Graves tells how Thomas Hardy had an idea for a story while he was gardening, 'the best he had ever conceived', complete with characters, setting, and even some dialogue. But when ready to write, a short time later, he was unable to recall any of his ideas. Hardy advised: 'Always carry a pencil and paper'.

We may think in words or picture situations in our imagination; and then use words to capture our thoughts and feelings for later consideration. Writing is therefore a creative process. The connection between writing and thinking is emphasised in the following quotations.

> Hardly any original thoughts on mental or social subjects ever make their way among mankind, or assume their proper importance in the minds even of their inventors, until aptly selected words or phrases have, as it were, nailed them down and held them fast.
>
> *A System of Logic*, John Stuart Mill (1875)

> The toil of writing and reconsideration may help to clear and fix many things that remain a little uncertain in my thoughts because they have never been fully stated, and I want to discover any lurking inconsistencies and unsuspected gaps. And I have a story.
>
> *The Passionate Friends*, H. G. Wells (1913)

When someone says 'I'm no good at English', what he or she really means is . . . 'I'm no good at thinking straight, I can't talk sense, I'm no good at being myself'.

English for Pleasure, L. A. G. Strong (1941)

An English course consisting only of grammar would be very barren, and command of language is best obtained by using it as a vehicle, for disciplining and recording thought and stimulating imaginative thinking.

The Language of Mathematics, F. W. Land (1975)

English is not like other school subjects: it is the condition of all academic life. The teaching of English is therefore the point at which all education must start.

Writing helps you to arrange your thoughts on any subject (see Table 2.1) and to plan your work (see chapter 4). Preparing an essay or project report makes you set down what you know and helps you to recognise gaps in your knowledge. This leads you to a deeper understanding of your work and is a stimulus to further study.

Writing helps you to communicate

Before the invention of the telephone in 1875, and of radio in 1901, verbal communication with anyone out of earshot was possible only by writing. Now, although we can converse with people anywhere in the world and see one another on a screen as we speak, writing remains the more important means of communication.

If anything is agreed on the telephone, for example, it is advisable to confirm in writing exactly what was agreed so that both parties have a record of the conversation, and so that any misunderstandings can be corrected in further correspondence. Also, in preparing letters, reports, or any other written communications, there is more time for thought, for deciding what to say, and for deciding how best to say it, than would be possible in a telephone conversation. As a result, material can be presented in a more effective order than would be possible in an unrehearsed conversation. There is time to check and correct the first draft – and if necessary to produce a revised and improved communication.

It is also worth remembering that speech, whether in direct conversation, by telephone, or over the radio, is still speech and is not in itself an innovation. People were speaking for many thousands of years before they developed writing and it is only by writing, especially since the invention of the printing press about five hundred years ago, that a great literature has been achieved and science has become a world-wide endeavour. The development of writing was a great innovation, and it is still by writing, whether using a pen and paper or a computer keyboard and electronic media, that important communications are prepared – even if they are not delivered in writing but, for example, as songs, plays, speeches or talks.

Improve your writing

Listen and note

Your lecture notes help you to remember and are a basis for your further studies (see Table 2.1). They are not normally seen by your lecturers. However, at the start of a talk about communication skills, a tutor could say that the students' notes will be collected at the end of the class. The talk would then be a test of each student's ability to listen, to understand what was said, to recognise and note important points, and to record enough supporting detail. After looking through the notes, the tutor could try to clarify any misunderstandings and could discuss with those students who do not have a good record of the talk how they could improve their listening and note-making skills.

Observe and describe

A class of students may be asked to study and then describe a familiar object, or to observe and then describe an everyday event. Differences between the descriptions prepared by different students will result from differences in their perception of the object or event, and differences in their ability to remember what they saw or to find appropriate words to express their thoughts. Differences may also be due to bias – to each observer having preconceived ideas that stand in the way of accurate observation, interpretation and reporting. This exercise provides a basis for a class discussion on the importance of writing as an aid to observation, and on possible reasons for differences between their perceptions and descriptions of one object or event.

Think and write

Keep a few sheets of notepaper in your pocket, and a pen, so that you can make a note of otherwise fleeting thoughts (as suggested on page 17). Other suggestions on the use of writing as an aid to thinking are included at the end of chapter 4.

Read good prose

To improve your ability to communicate in writing, read good prose regularly – for example, read books by established authors and leading articles in good newspapers. However, do not attempt to copy anyone else's style. As your use of words improves you will continue to develop your own style of writing that reflects your own personality and your feeling for words.

3 How students should write

In a novel or short story it is not necessary to explain everything. The writing is subjective – based on the imagination. In contrast, the written work of most students, most of the time, is objective – based on things we can observe with our five senses, which we think of as facts.

Use words to convey your thoughts

Essential characteristics of scholarly writing

Your purpose as a student, and in most professions, will be to communicate information and ideas clearly – with nothing left to the imagination. To help you think about the essential characteristics of such scholarly writing, consider what you would expect of a set of instructions. We all use instructions: how to bake a cake, how to write an essay. What are your requirements when using instructions?

Explanation

What are the instructions for? Their purpose must be made clear in an informative title or heading. What materials do you need to complete the task? In a recipe the ingredients are listed immediately after the heading. What do you have to do? The set of instructions must be a clear explanation.

Order

You will expect the task to be broken into separate steps, with each step distinct and the steps arranged in the right order – the order in which things have to be done – and preferably numbered so that you know you have completed one step before you proceed to the next.

Clarity

Each instruction must be a complete and carefully constructed unambiguous sentence, so that the action required at each step cannot be misunderstood.

Relevance

Only the information needed to help you complete the task should be provided. Similarly, in any composition, only material relevant to the title or to the question being answered should be included.

Simplicity

Any unnecessary words could be confusing (see Figure 3.1).

Completeness

If an essential step were omitted you would be unable, by following the instructions, to complete the task.

Accuracy

You will expect the writer to have worked through the instructions while performing the task, to check that there were no mistakes.

The need for sufficient explanation, the orderly presentation of the material, clarity, relevance, simplicity, completeness and accuracy is most obvious in preparing instructions, but these things are essential in all except imaginative writing.

The writing of all considerate writers, who in helping their readers by conveying information and ideas clearly and pleasurably also help themselves, has all these and other characteristics (listed alphabetically, not in order of importance, in Table 3.1).

> All the virtues of language are, in their roots, moral; it becomes accurate if the speaker desires to be true; clear, if he speaks with sympathy and a desire to be intelligible; powerful, if he has earnestness; pleasant, if he has a sense of rhythm and order. There are no other virtues of language producible by art than these; . . .
>
> Ruskin (quoted by Sampson, 1925, page 70)

'Tell them to send shorter messages!'

Figure 3.1 Keep all communications short and to the point

Present the results of your own thinking

Originality

The work you present for assessment as a student, in coursework and examinations, must be the results of your own thinking. Like any other document that you write under your own name, or to which you put your signature, it must be your own work. This fact may seem so obvious to you as to go without saying; but it is important to recognise that the submission of work that is not original in this sense can result in disciplinary proceedings against the student or students concerned.

Cheating

Submitting work done by anyone else as your own work (for example, a composition written by a friend or downloaded from an internet site) would be cheating and is obviously unacceptable. Other serious disciplinary offences, which are examples of dishonesty and cheating, are plagiarism, collusion, and fabrication.

Higher education establishments have strict rules and regulations relating to the various forms of cheating, and to the abuse and misuse of communications and information technology. Clear guidance is made available to all new students, for example in a student handbook or course guide, and any student provided with such information will be assumed to have read it and to be aware of any rules and regulations it contains.

Plagiarism

Just as it is unacceptable to copy from any composition prepared by another student, so it is unacceptable to copy material from any publication, or from the internet, and include it in your own compositions without proper acknowledgement. This would be plagiarism: stealing someone else's thoughts. You must not do this deliberately; and you must take great care to ensure that you do not do it inadvertently (for example, as a result of cutting sentences from electronic sources and pasting them into your own notes).

Even if you summarise someone else's published thoughts, opinions or findings, in your own words, you must record your source in your notes. Then if you include such material in assessed coursework, or in any other composition you present as your own, you must include an appropriate acknowledgement of each source. For advice on how to do this, see *Cite sources of information* (pages 132–3), *List your sources of information* (page 134), and *Acknowledgements* in Table 11.1.

Collusion

Collaboration in a project or in group work may be an essential part of your course, to encourage the sharing of ideas and team work; and in preparing any assignment you can benefit from discussing your work with other people. But having co-operated in such work you must evaluate the information you have obtained from different sources, decide what to include and how best to arrange your material, and write by yourself any composition you submit for assessment as your own work: making clear your knowledge of the subject, your interpretation of evidence, your reasoning, your understanding, and your conclusions.

Table 3.1 Some characteristics of scholarly writing

Characteristic	Explanation
accuracy*	
appropriateness	to the subject, to the reader, and to the occasion
balance	showing an awareness of all sides of a question; maintaining a sense of proportion
clarity*	
completeness*	
consistency	in the use of numbers, names, abbreviations, spelling, punctuation, etc.
control	paying careful attention to arrangement, presentation and timing – so as to affect the reader in a chosen way
explanation*	
impartiality	unbiased by preconceived ideas
interest	holding the reader's attention
objectivity	with all conclusions based on evidence, not on unsupported opinion
order*	
originality*	
persuasiveness	convincing the reader by evidence and argument
precision	exact definition supported, as appropriate, by counting or by accurate measurement
relevance*	with no irrelevant material
simplicity*	
sincerity	the quality of frankness, honesty
unity	the quality of wholeness, coherence

Note
* See sub-headings in this chapter.

Fabrication

Most scholarly writing is objective (mainly factual), not subjective (based mainly on the imagination). The material you present as fact must not be fiction. It must be based on things you have seen for yourself and recorded as data (for example, in field or laboratory practical work), or on information recorded by other people (facts and interpretations from the sources cited in your composition). Fabrication, the inclusion of thoughts that are mere products of the imagination, whether expressed in words, diagrams or as numbers, is unacceptable.

Improve your writing

Always prepare your work carefully.

1   Include sufficient explanation.

2   Arrange the parts of your composition in an appropriate order, to suit your purpose.
3   Make your meaning clear throughout, so that no sentence can be misunderstood.
4   Convey your message as clearly and simply as you can (see Figure 3.1).
5   Make sure your work is complete: with nothing your readers need to know omitted.
6   Check your work carefully. Try to ensure that every statement is correct.

Prepare a set of instructions

Preparing a set of instructions is a good test of your ability to communicate effectively. Prepare a set of instructions on how to replace the batteries in a portable radio, or on how to complete some other simple task. Then try to perform the task, following your own instructions. If necessary revise your instructions. Then ask someone else to undertake the task, to see if they can complete the task satisfactorily by following your instructions or suggest any improvements.

You may find, if you look at a portable radio, that instructions on how to change the batteries are provided – perhaps just by including a simple diagram. Why is it desirable to convey such information without words?

A more interesting exercise, in which members of a discussion group can work first alone, then in pairs, and then in groups of four (as small committees) is to write a set of instructions headed *How to write a set of instructions*. As a class exercise, this is perhaps best undertaken before considering the essential characteristics of scholarly writing (see pages 21–5).

Read critically

The word criticise does not mean 'find fault with'. A theatre critic could report that a new play was excellent and say what was good about it, or at the other extreme advise – with reasons – why the play was not worth seeing. Most critics would write something about the plot, and about the acting, stating what they liked and commenting on aspects of the performance they consider could be improved, so that readers could decide for themselves whether or not they were likely to enjoy the play.

Develop your own ability to think critically. Do not believe, without question, everything you see in print, or take for granted that the author's is the only possible point of view. Consider whether or not the author tells you everything you would like to know. Criticising the work of others should help you to recognise good writing, and so to improve your own written work.

Unclear, imprecise and unnecessarily complex writing is to be found in the most unexpected places. Read critically each of the following extracts, from a book or magazine, noting any questions or comments that come to mind. Then consider the faults listed and the suggestions as to how each extract could have been revised and improved.

Extract from a geography textbook

Much of the Romagna of Italy, for instance, which was fully populated in ancient times, was only restored to its ancient population and productivity by great efforts in the present century.

SOME FAULTS	COMMENTS
1 fully populated in ancient times	This is imprecise. How many people? When?
2 only restored . . . by	This should read: restored . . . only by
3 to its ancient population	Very old people?
4 and productivity	As productive as in ancient times?

Extract from a book on examination technique

The complaints of examiners that students cannot write good English applies, I think, mainly to science students. Now science is founded on mathematics, and in general it is found that those who have an ability for literature are poor mathematicians and vice versa . . . As their abilities lie outside literature it is not surprising that science students write badly.

SOME FAULTS

1 The author should have written either that the complaints . . . apply, or that the complaint . . . applies.

2 in the second sentence, the repetition of sound and of cognate forms in different parts of speech (*founded* on . . . is *found* that . . .) offends the ear (see page 105).

3 The author is inconsistent: an opinion expressed in the first sentence is stated as a fact in the third.

4 The author makes the vague statement 'in general it is found that' but gives no evidence in support of this generalisation. In fact, some science students write well and some students of literature (see page 5) and some literary critics (see page 28) write badly. Many people are good at both arts and science subjects. No students need feel discouraged: the more effort they put into any subject the more they will understand and enjoy it.

Extract from a magazine article by a professor of education

The last ten years or so have seen changes in teaching of a magnitude unequalled in any previous period of our educational history. Such advances have necessitated a monumental expenditure of money and human resources, and it is interesting to note that whereas in countries like the United States . . .

SOME FAULTS

1   *Of a magnitude unequalled* means unequalled (see Table 6.4).
2   *In any previous period of our educational history* means either in our educational history or, more probably, in any ten-year period (see Table 5.4).
3   The changes mentioned in the first sentence are called advances in the second sentence (see *progress*, page 59).
4   Advances do not necessitate.
5   Expenditure cannot be monumental.
6   The words *it is interesting to note that* can be omitted without altering the meaning of this sentence (see Table 4.1).
7   Are any countries like the United States? The author means in some countries, including the United States . . .

Extract from a learned journal

Safe and efficient driving is a matter of living up to the psychological laws of locomotion in a spatial field. The driver's field of safe travel and his minimum stopping zone must accord with the objective possibilities; and a ratio greater than unity must be maintained between them. This is the basic principle. High speed, slippery road, night driving, sharp curves, heavy traffic and the like are dangerous, when they are, because they lower the field zone ratio.

SOME FAULTS

1   The writer's meaning is not clear. Does this extract mean that a driver should always be able to stop within the distance that can be seen to be clear?
2   The writer seems to have tried to make a simple subject unnecessarily complex.

Maugham (1938) in *The Summing Up* says that many people write obscurely because they have never taken the trouble to learn to write clearly – even literary critics whom, having passed their lives in the study of great literature, one would expect to be sufficiently sensitive to the beauty of language to write, if not beautifully, at least with perspicuity. 'Yet you will find in their works sentence after sentence that you must read twice in order to discover the sense. Often you can only guess at it, for the writers have evidently not said what they intended.'

Maugham suggests that another cause of obscurity is that the writers themselves are not quite sure of their meaning. Many have only a vague impression of what they want to say, because they think not before they write but as they write – and so cannot be expected to find precise expression for their confused ideas.

Practise writing

To be good at any game, or to play any musical instrument well, you must practise regularly. Similarly, to write well you must practise writing: for example, by keeping a private diary in which you record your own experiences or by corresponding regularly with a friend. Each time you write, take the trouble to convey your thoughts in carefully constructed unambiguous sentences, arranged in an appropriate order, and organised in paragraphs, so that you can understand your personal records later, and so that each communication will be understood at first reading by the reader you have in mind.

Just as in playing a game you can learn to play better by watching the best players, so your own writing will improve if you read leading articles in quality newspapers and books by authors who write well. And you can learn by considering the advice of experienced and successful authors:

> Write as simply as you can – as though you were writing a letter to a friend.
>
> William Somerset Maugham

> Write as often as possible. Read good authors critically . . . noticing how they work.
>
> J. B. Priestley

> Never copy other writers. Never wait for inspiration. Get something down on paper . . . and look at it the next morning to see how you can improve it.
>
> Nicholas Monserrat

> Success depends upon natural talent developed by hard work.
>
> Evelyn Waugh

If you write badly it is probably because you have not thought sufficiently about what you want to say. To write well, write about things you know best and try to express your thoughts as clearly and simply as you can. Always think before you begin.

1   Whom do you expect to interest?
2   What do they need to know?
3   How best can you tell them?

4 Answering questions in coursework

When you write, unless you are just taking notes, you are composing: expressing your own thoughts in your own way. A letter to a friend; a written answer to a question in coursework or examinations; a memorandum to a colleague in business, management, production or research; a report in a newspaper or a project report; an essay or article in a magazine or journal: all these are compositions.

The first step towards better writing is to recognise the possibility of improvement. Then to ensure continuing improvement, and so provide encouragement, prepare every composition – however small – in four stages. Always: think, plan, write, and then check your work.

The first two stages – thinking and planning – will help you to make a start and take you well on the way to completing your work. In an examination only a few minutes can be devoted to thinking and planning, but in coursework much time may be spent on the search for information and ideas, and in discussion and thought. But, irrespective of the time available, you must first consider what exactly is required.

Think about the question

In coursework your title will be the question you must answer. You should be given this in writing so that there is no possibility of misunderstandings. However, if the question is dictated in class do not take it down in note form or rely on another student to record it for you. To ensure accuracy, write every word and punctuation mark carefully yourself.

A good title will inform the reader, but before this it should enable you to define the purpose and scope of your composition. In preparing any communication the most important consideration is not what you know but what your readers need to know. In coursework and examinations each of your compositions will be seen by only one assessor who will require *your* answer to the questions set: no more, no less.

Analyse the question

The wording of the question, your terms of reference, or the title, should concentrate your attention on the needs of the assessor. The most common faults in students' written work, if they know their subject, are failure to answer precisely the question set and the inclusion of irrelevant material. Some students read the question and immediately start to write all they know about the subject. It is as if they expected the assessor to search for relevant material. But anything irrelevant – sometimes called padding – is likely to obscure meaning. It makes clear only that the writer did not understand exactly what was required. By making relevant material harder to locate, any superfluous words or phrases actually make it harder for an assessor to award marks.

To make yourself think about exactly what is required, so that you include only relevant material, analyse each question in four stages before you plan your answer. The initial letters S A R I will help you to remember the four stages.

S	*Subject*	What is the question about?
A	*Aspect*	Which aspect or aspects of the subject must be included in your answer to this question? You are unlikely to be asked to write all you know about any subject.
R	*Restrictions*	Do any words limit the scope of your answer (for example: brief, concise, outline)?
I	*Instructions*	Which words are instructions (for example: compare, essay, explain, summarise)? See also *Understand the words used in questions* (page 67).

It will not take you long to analyse each question you are asked, in this way, to ensure that you respond to its exact wording when planning your answer.

Stimulate your thoughts

Make notes as you analyse the question. Record relevant thoughts as they come to mind. Spread key words, phrases and sentences over a sheet of paper (or over the whole of your computer screen), leaving plenty of space for additions. Note your main points as headings (usually by selecting words from different parts of the question) and note supporting details below each heading.

The person marking your work, like any other reader, wants relevant information and ideas well organised and clearly presented.

In an *argument* you must provide evidence, in an appropriate order, supported if necessary by examples, referring to possible interpretations of the evidence and opinions, and ending with your conclusions.

In a *description* your purpose is to produce in the mind of the reader a picture of the scene, object or event observed (using your five senses). You should proceed from its general characteristics to details: from the general to the particular (as with a definition, see page 68), or perhaps beginning with things perceived from the outside (for example, of a building, or of a piece of equipment).

In *narration* (writing a story) the reader needs to know what happened (in chronological order), when, where, and who was involved, with some description; and would like to know how it happened and why.

In *exposition* (explanation) the reader may need to know, for example, what it is, who may find it useful, and how it works.

Whatever you are writing, ask yourself the six questions your reader would ask in conversation – What? Why? When? How? Where? Who?

Add to your notes as you think of the answers to these questions, which serve as mental tin-openers. As you make notes you will think of other questions, and your answers will allow you to make more notes.

Another way to stimulate your thoughts is to consider the different subjects in your course of study. Are any relevant to this composition? Be prepared to bring together information and ideas from different sources. Different lecturers are concerned with different aspects of your course, but information and ideas should be integrated in your mind, in your notes, in your contributions to discussions, and in your written answers to questions set in coursework and examinations.

After a few minutes of thought and reflection, or longer if you have time, you will find you know much more about many topics than you supposed when first reading many of the questions set as coursework assignments or on examination papers. If you were writing a letter to a friend or a report for an employer you would probably omit anything you expected the reader to know already. But as a student, writing anything that is to be assessed, you must display your knowledge and understanding. You cannot omit definitions or important details because they seem obvious to you. Every question set is a test of your knowledge and understanding of an aspect of your subject, of your ability to make use of appropriate sources of information, and of your ability to think critically and then present your thoughts in an organised (well structured) answer that makes clear your knowledge and understanding.

Plan your answer

The notes made as you think about a question are useful when you start to plan your answer. You may select some as topics for separate paragraphs and others as supporting points to be made in different paragraphs. You may omit some, in your final selection of material, either because they provide unnecessary detail or because you choose better examples.

Select effective headings

Read the question again, carefully. Ensure: (a) that the headings in your notes are appropriate and do signpost all parts of the question, (b) that you do answer all parts of the question, and (c) that you answer them in an effective order – normally the order in which they appear in the question.

Headings are essential in your plan. They help you to think about the question, to ensure that you answer all parts of the question, to get things into an effective order, to avoid repetition, and to check that everything included is relevant not only to the question as a whole but also to the preceding heading. Good headings and sub-headings are essential in most long compositions. They provide signposts for readers, but it is best not to use them in literary compositions (for example, essays in English literature), and some lecturers may advise you not to use them in any short composition. Also, what is encouraged in some subjects may be discouraged in others. Use them in your plan, but not necessarily in your answer.

Prepare a plan of your answer: a topic outline

Making notes spread over a whole sheet of paper (or on your computer screen) enables you to record relevant thoughts. Then, perhaps in a later study session when you have had time to find the additional information you need on any topic, you can reconsider your notes and organise them into a plan or topic outline as you make the following decisions.

1   How will you introduce the subject? In most compositions a short crisp first paragraph is needed to capture the reader's interest.
2   What is the topic for each of the other paragraphs?
3   What supporting information and ideas should be included in each paragraph?
4   Which of your notes should be deleted because, on second thoughts, you decide they provide unnecessary detail or are not relevant, or because you have chosen better examples?

5   What needs emphasis? Underline these points in your plan (but not in your composition – see page 104).
6   Are any tables or diagrams needed? If they are, where should they be placed in your composition? Knowing this, you can number them, include each one near the most appropriate paragraph and refer to it in this paragraph and if necessary in other, usually later, paragraphs.
7   In what order should the paragraphs be arranged to serve your purpose?
8   What would be a suitable conclusion? Normally your last paragraph should be short and to the point.

Number your paragraphs as you decide on the most appropriate order (or rearrange them on your computer screen) so that you can use your plan as a guide to both the order of paragraphs and the content of each paragraph as you write your answer.

These decisions about content and arrangement, made as you prepare your plan, provide a definite structure for your composition that will make for easy reading: enabling you to communicate information and ideas forcefully yet pleasurably. More than this, such a well-structured composition that displays your knowledge and understanding – your mastery of the subject – will help you to interest and convince an assessor, and score high marks.

The principles of composition are the same whether you use a pen or a word processor. The only difference in organising your thoughts is that with pen and paper you number the topics in your plan as you decide on the order of paragraphs, whereas on a computer screen you can drag your notes into an appropriate order as you decide on both the order of paragraphs and the content of each paragraph.

However, one advantage of preparing your topic outline on paper is that (as when using a laptop) you can work anywhere. Another, if you make a habit of planning and writing a first draft on paper, is that you will not be at a disadvantage when you have only a pen and paper (for example, as a student, in an examination).

In an examination you may be able to spare only a few minutes for thinking about a question and planning your answer, but as a result you will be able to write faster – once you start – and you will probably write more than if you had started to write immediately after reading the question (with insufficient thought). Your answer will also be better organised, easier to mark, more direct, more nearly complete, and likely to score higher marks than would a less well considered composition.

In coursework you are advised to spend five or ten minutes thinking about a question, and making relevant notes soon after the question is set – perhaps on the same evening. Think again on the next day and spend fifteen minutes adding to your notes and making them into a topic outline. This may draw your attention to topics about which you need further information before you can start writing: make a note of these. Thinking and planning in this way, before you look at your lecture notes, your textbook, or other sources of information (see chapter 9, *Finding and using information*) will serve to direct your attention to what is needed to answer each question and help you to prepare a unique answer (your answer) that is based on your own thought and is not just a rehash of things heard in lectures or read in a book (see *Originality*, page 23).

Always think and plan first, and only then refer to other sources of information – and if necessary revise your plan. When you are happy with your plan, put it on one side for a while. This will enable you to think again, clarify your ideas, find additional information, and if necessary revise your plan. At this stage read the question again. Your plan should include all the points you consider necessary, in an appropriate order, as a basis for a balanced answer to the question set. Your aim should be to prepare a topic outline similar to the assessor's marking scheme – to be used in marking your work. It is easier to add new topics to your outline, or to change the order of presentation of material at this stage (even when using a word processor), than it would be to change your mind after you have started to write.

Maintain order

Aristotle in *Poetics* said of a drama that it must have a beginning, a middle and an end. So must any letter, any essay-type answer to a question set in coursework or in an examination, any dissertation or thesis, or any other document or report.

Each composition may be compared to an old-fashioned railway train, with an engine, a number of carriages and a guard's van. In any composition, the first paragraph (the introduction) and the last paragraph (the conclusion) serve different purposes, resulting from their positions at the beginning and at the end (like the engine and the guard's van). Each of the other paragraphs is distinct, but as part of the whole (like each carriage of the train) it links what has gone before to what is to follow.

After the title and the introductory paragraph, further paragraphs should be arranged in an appropriate order so that they lead smoothly to the closing paragraph. An appropriate order may be, for example, the logical steps in an argument, a chronological order, or one geographical region after another. In a short work it may be an order of increasing importance, and in a long work an order of decreasing importance.

The first paragraph is your readers' first taste of what is to come. Here you must capture their interest. Your first paragraph must leave no doubt as to the purpose and scope of the composition (if this is not stated in the title). In coursework or examinations it should be apparent that you have begun to answer the question set; and that paragraph may be the gist of your answer. However, there are many ways of beginning (see *How to begin*, page 102).

There should be one paragraph for each of the topics included in your composition, so that – as far as possible – you can say in one place all you need to say about each of the points you need to make. Like the composition as a whole, each paragraph should have a beginning, a middle and an end. That is to say, the sentences should be well ordered. Each one should be clearly relevant, with a limited and well-defined purpose.

The topic for each paragraph is usually clearly stated (or is apparent) in the first sentence; but in an explanation or argument the topic sentence may come last. All sentences in the paragraph should show your understanding of the topic. They may provide relevant information (ideas, evidence, an explanation or an example) and the first and last sentences should also help to link the paragraphs so that the reader is led smoothly on from one paragraph to the next. This is one reason why, although it is easy to cut and paste paragraphs when word processing, if the order of paragraphs is changed (when writing or revising any composition) the wording of every paragraph must be reconsidered to ensure that every sentence still makes sense, and that no words or paragraphs are out of place.

Because the first and last words in a paragraph attract most attention, never begin a paragraph with unimportant words. Omit superfluous introductory phrases such as First let us consider . . . Secondly it must be stated that . . . An interesting example which should be mentioned in this context is . . . Next it must be noted that . . . It goes without saying that . . . We can sum up by saying that . . .

Such thoughts should be going through your mind as you prepare your topic outline. They are an aid to thinking and planning. How shall I begin? What should I say next? Then what? Should I omit this? How shall I conclude? These questions will help you to put your thoughts (and your paragraphs) into an appropriate order, but they are not for your readers (who require only the results of your thinking). Superfluous introductory and connecting phrases (see also Tables 4.1 and 4.2), like any other unnecessary words, merely distract a reader's attention from your message.

The change from one topic to the next should be signposted by a clear break between paragraphs. In a handwritten composition the first words of each paragraph, apart from the introductory paragraph, should be indented. In a word-processed composition, with single spacing, one line should be left blank between paragraphs (and with double spacing two lines blank).

Table 4.1 Introductory and connecting phrases that can usually be omitted without altering the meaning of the sentence*

It is considered in this connection that . . .
From this point of view, it is relevant to mention that . . .
In regard to . . . when we consider . . . it is apparent that . . .
As far as . . . is concerned, it may be noted that . . .
It is of interest to note that . . . of course . . .
From this information it is clear that . . .
It has been established that, essentially . . . in the *case* of . . .
In the *field* of . . . for your information . . . in actual *fact* . . .
with reference to . . . in the last analysis

Note
*   The abstract nouns printed in italics are indicators of jargon.

After the paragraph break the reader is expecting a new topic, and the first sentence in most paragraphs is the topic sentence. The new topic is introduced directly and forcefully, usually in the first few words.

Within a paragraph, each sentence should convey one thought, or a few closely related thoughts. Punctuation marks should be used only when they are needed to clarify meaning or make for easy reading (see punctuation, pages 193–6). Each sentence should be obviously related to the preceding sentence and to the next. No new statement should be introduced abruptly and without warning. The sentences in each paragraph should therefore be in an effective order so that they hold together, develop a train of thought, and convey your meaning precisely.

Balance is important in writing, as in most things. The sentences in a paragraph and the paragraphs in any communication, like the handle and the blade of a knife, must be balanced in themselves and in relation to one another. Your composition as a whole must be well balanced, with ideas of comparable importance given similar emphasis.

Paragraphing breaks up the page of writing, provides pauses at appropriate points in your composition, and helps the reader to know when it is time to pass from one topic to the next. Short paragraphs are the easiest to read and make for efficient communication, but paragraphs are units of thought – each with one or a few closely connected thoughts – and they will therefore vary in length.

Only you can decide if your composition is so long that the reader needs a summary; but a short composition prepared in an examination or in answer to a question set as coursework should not normally end with a summary. You should be able to make better use of your final paragraph: it is your chance to affect the reader in a chosen way. Topics covered in your

Table 4.2 Introductory phrases that should usually be deleted

Introductory phrase	A possible interpretation
Arguably	I do not wish to commit myself
As is well known	I think
It is evident that	I think
It is perhaps true to say that	I do not know what to think
It is generally agreed that	Some people think
All reasonable people think	I believe
For obvious reasons,	I can't remember why, but
There is no doubt that	I am convinced
To be honest	I do not always tell the truth
With respect	I think you are talking nonsense
It is not necessary to stress the fact that	I should not need to tell you this
As mentioned earlier	I have already told you this
As you know	This is superfluous

preceding paragraphs should have led to your conclusion; or they should have provided a basis for speculation; or they should allow you to emphasise some aspect of the subject which serves to link all paragraphs. Whatever method you adopt for bringing your composition to a close, the end should be obvious to the reader. It should not be necessary to begin the closing paragraph, as so many inexperienced writers do, with the words 'In conclusion . . .'

Tichy and Fourdrinier (1988) emphasise that in a well-organised composition:

> Good paragraphs . . . vary in length, development, and organisation. They move . . . quickly through simple material and explain . . . any difficult points. Good paragraphs are carefully connected, and when there is a marked change in thought, there are enough indications to help readers follow the shift. Good paragraphs do not repeat unnecessarily or digress; instead they cover their subjects thoroughly and briefly. While their readers are still interested, the writing ends in a satisfactory final paragraph . . .

Write your answer

Write in your own words

In any answer you prepare in coursework or in examinations it is essential to show an awareness of relevant material explained in lectures or discussed in seminars and tutorials that have formed part of your course. It is not usual to acknowledge these sources of information and ideas but it would obviously be a mistake to ignore things your lecturers consider important – especially if these lecturers will also assess your work.

From the start of your course make use of the other sources of information and ideas recommended by your lecturers and tutors to support their lectures, seminars, tutorials and other group work. And before reading any book, or other publication, always record its full bibliographic details at the start of any notes you make (see page 128). Then you will be able to acknowledge the source of any published material referred to in your own compositions.

Background reading is important as a way of obtaining additional information on any subject, a different approach, different interpretations of evidence, and new ideas. But it should be a stimulus to your thinking – not an alternative to thinking for yourself. You could not produce an original answer to a question simply by copying relevant sentences from your lecture notes or, if it were acceptable, from a textbook (see *Originality*, page 23). Also, each writer has a different style of writing and if material were to be taken from different sources the changes in style would be obvious to a discriminating reader and would make for hard reading.

The time you spend thinking and planning will help you to write a better answer than would otherwise have been possible. With your topic outline before you, as a guide, you can write with the whole composition in mind. Knowing how you will introduce the subject, the order of paragraphs, and how you will end, you can: (a) begin well, (b) maintain order, (c) make connections to help the reader follow your train of thought, (d) avoid repetition by dealing with each topic fully in one paragraph, (e) ensure relevance, (f) emphasise your main points, (g) write quickly, and (h) arrive at an effective conclusion. In short, guided by your topic outline – your plan – you maintain control and produce an original composition.

Write at one sitting

Your topic outline will be useful if you are unable to complete your composition at one sitting – because of its length, or an unforeseen interruption, or the pressure of other work. Many professional people write in a busy office or in places where they are constantly interrupted by enquiries from colleagues, by telephone conversations, and because they must attend to other tasks.

Similarly, as a student you get used to working in a library where there may be distractions. Perhaps you read each day on a train as you travel to and from college, or you work on a topic outline for a short time between other tasks. However, if possible, when you have finished thinking and planning and are ready to write, try to put other work on one side and write where you will be free from interruptions or other distractions (see Figure 8.1).

With your topic outline complete, the theme chosen, and the end in sight, try to write at one sitting. Use the words that first come to mind. Stopping for conversation, or to revise sentences already written, or to check the spelling of a word, or to search for a better word, may interrupt the flow of ideas and so destroy the spontaneity that gives freshness, interest and unity to a composition. The time for revising your work is when the first draft is complete.

Use your topic outline as a guide. Present information in a well-ordered, interesting and straightforward way. Use enough words to make your meaning clear. Too few words will provide insufficient explanation and too many may obscure meaning and will waste the reader's time.

Base your arguments in favour of any ideas you express on evidence summarised in your composition. Where appropriate, support your statements with examples so that the reader can judge their validity. Base any adverse criticism of other people's work on reasoned argument, not on preconceived ideas for which you are unable to find supporting evidence.

Check your answer

Two processes are involved in written communication. The first, in your mind, is the selection of words to express your thoughts and feelings. The second is the interpretation of these words by each of your readers. The essential difficulty is in trying to ensure that you affect readers as you intended: creating in the mind of each reader thoughts and feelings identical with those that were in your mind (see Figure 4.1).

Too often, the reader is confronted by an ambiguous sentence or a statement that is obviously incorrect and has to try to work out what the writer probably meant. So, always check your compositions carefully to try to ensure that your words do record your thoughts unambiguously and that readers will find them easy to read and understand. Usually in scholarly writing you will be concerned with your knowledge of a subject and with communicating information, not with stirring the emotions.

A common failing in writing is to include things in one part of a composition that would be better placed in another part. Indeed, one of the most difficult tasks is to arrange all that is to be said in the most effective order. One reason for this, even after careful planning, is that we remember relevant points as we write. Information and ideas may then be included in one paragraph even though they would be better placed in another.

In writing we use words as they come to mind, but our first thoughts are

1 Sender	Communication	2 Receiver
THOUGHTS --------	MESSAGE --------	THOUGHTS
FEELINGS		FEELINGS

Figure 4.1 Written communication involves the choice of words to convey your thoughts as a message in an attempt to evoke identical thoughts in the mind of the reader

not necessarily our best thoughts – and they may not be arranged in the most effective order. Wrong words and words out of place will distract attention from your message, and may result in ambiguity. Like inappropriate words, unsuited to their context, to the reader, or to the occasion, they are barriers to easy communication.

By further thought, a writer should be able to improve a first draft. If possible, therefore, put your composition on one side for at least a day. Then check it carefully, correcting any mistakes. Revise it, if necessary, to ensure that your readers do not have to waste their time on an uncorrected first draft – which otherwise may reflect neither your intentions nor your ability. Read the whole composition aloud to ensure that it sounds well and that you have not written words or clumsy expressions you would not use in speech.

To admit that you need to plan your work and that you can improve your first draft is not to say that you are unintelligent. The apparent spontaneity of easy-reading prose is the result of hard work (see Table 4.5). Intelligence and effort are needed if a subject is to be presented as simply as possible. Simplicity in writing, as in a mathematical proof, is the outward sign of clarity of thought.

Every writer should check and, if necessary, should correct and improve the first draft. Flaubert (1821–80) had high self-imposed standards. He worked for hours at each page: writing, rewriting, reading aloud, recasting, trying to achieve perfection. Colette (1873–1954) wrote everything over and over again and would spend a whole morning working on one page. Somerset Maugham (1874–1965) said that if he achieved the effect of ease in his writing, it was only by strenuous effort. H. G. Wells (1866–1946) would write a first draft that was full of gaps, and then make changes between the lines and in the margin. Aldous Huxley (1894–1963) said, 'All my thoughts are second thoughts'.

Those who write best probably spend the most time criticising and revising their prose, making it clear and concise but not stultified – and ensuring the smooth flow of language. However, revision must not be taken too far – so that this natural flow is lost. Alan Sillitoe said of *Saturday Night and Sunday Morning*: 'It had been turned down by several publishers but I had written it eight times, polished it, and could only spoil it by touching it again'.

As a result of thinking and planning before you start to write, there should not be much wrong with any composition. And as a student you do not want to get into the habit of writing coursework assignments more than once: you will not have time to rewrite your answers in examinations. However, you should always check your coursework to see if you could improve it – and should be prepared to rewrite any composition if you decide that by doing so you can express your thoughts more effectively, and make it easier to read and mark. Even in examinations you should allow time to check each answer – to make good any important omissions and to correct any obvious mistakes or slips of the pen.

The pleasure to be derived from writing comes from the effort of creative activity – which should help you to learn about the subject of each composition and lead you to a deeper understanding. Each composition, prepared as suggested in this chapter, is an original work: it is a vehicle for self-expression that involves you in organising your thoughts and then presenting information and ideas *in your own way*. No one else would select the same material for inclusion, arrange arguments in the same way, make the same criticisms, or reach the same conclusions.

Pleasure comes from writing something that will affect other people. A reader may be persuaded or convinced by logical argument and evidence clearly presented, or may be misled and annoyed by poor writing. Each communication is a challenge to you to present information and ideas directly and forcefully, to help the reader along, and *to affect the reader in a chosen way* – for this is the purpose of all exposition.

Presentation is important. A well-presented composition makes an immediate favourable impression on the reader; but consider what is involved in good presentation (see Table 4.3). Do not waste your time on mere decoration, which can do nothing to make good any deficiencies in other respects and which *should* have little or no influence on the mark awarded (see Table 4.4).

The world may be impressed by outward show, but assessors in higher education and professional people in other employment should not be deceived by ornament. Neither neat handwriting nor the clear print of a word-processed document can make up for deficiencies in other respects: for example, from an inability to use language confidently and correctly, or from the use of inappropriate headings, or from the inclusion of information or ideas that are inappropriate, irrelevant or out of place.

You are advised not to word-process all your coursework assignments,

Table 4.3 Ensure your work is well presented

---

1   Write legibly or use a word processor (see chapter 13, *Your computer as an aid to writing*).
2   Start with your name, the date and the title (see pages 22 and 50).
3   Use appropriate subheadings if these will help the reader (see pages 34 and 103).
4   Leave a clear break between paragraphs (see pages 37 and 38) and ensure an orderly arrangement of paragraphs (see page 36) with no paragraph too long (see page 38).
5   Arrange sentences effectively in each paragraph (see page 38).
6   Ensure each sentence is grammatically correct and unambiguous.
7   Use no more words than are needed to express your thoughts clearly and simply (see pages 72–8).
8   Use punctuation marks to help readers understand each sentence at first reading (see chapter 14, *What is the point?: A quick guide to punctuation*).
9   Check the spelling of any word, if you are not sure it is correct (see chapter 15, *Spelling check*).
10 Number the pages.

---

unless you are required to do so, just because you think print looks more impressive than handwriting. Even if you are required to submit course-work that has been word processed, it is important that you should be used to handwriting at least the first draft of each of your compositions in the time that would have been available for the composition in an examination, unless you will also be able to use a word processor in examinations.

Anyone who is unable to touch type is handicapped when using a computer for word processing (see *Improving your keyboard skills*, page 182). And some students are handicapped by slow handwriting because, having been taught to print each letter separately when they were learning to write, they have not progressed to joined-up writing in which the pen runs smoothly from letter to letter without a pause or break in the line until the word is complete.

In answering questions in coursework it is best to maintain and develop the ability to write quickly with a pen on wide-lined A4 paper, with a 25 mm ruled margin, similar to the paper provided for your answers in examinations. In examinations, having spent time on thinking and planning, before writing, you will want to be able to write legibly and as fast as you can. Legible writing is an essential part of good presentation (see Table 4.3); and, obviously, words that cannot be read cannot score marks.

Assess your answer

For the person assessing your work, the thoughts you express and the way your answer is organised are the only guides to the quality of your thinking.

Table 4.4 Scoring marks for a written answer as part of a degree course

Standard of work Grade	Mark out of ten	
Outstanding *Presentation.* Work neat, well organised, and clearly expressed. *Length.* Appropriate. *Content.* Displaying knowledge and understanding of all aspects of a complete and correct answer to the question asked. Probably including information and ideas gained by reading beyond standard texts, knowledge of recent work, and, for the highest marks, original ideas.	8+	A
Good Displaying knowledge of most or all aspects of a complete answer, but understanding not always made clear, and perhaps giving no indication of background reading. Perhaps longer than is necessary and including some irrelevant material.	6 +	B
Average *Answer incomplete:* does not include all essentials. Unnecessary repetition and poor organisation may indicate an incomplete grasp of the subject, or an inability to communicate effectively. May include irrelevant material, indicating that the question was not properly understood.	5	C
Just acceptable	4	D
Answer inaccurate or incomplete. Not up to the required standard.	3	F
Displaying little knowledge and no understanding.	2	F
Displaying no knowledge or including only irrelevant material.	0	F

Source: Barrass, R. (2002) *Study! A Guide to Effective Learning, Revision and Examination Techniques*, 2nd edition, London, Routledge

When the question is set you may be provided with information about how it will be assessed – explaining what is expected if a student is to achieve a particular grade. These assessment and grading criteria may apply to a particular question only, or they may be expressed in general terms (as in Table 4.4) so that they apply to any question that requires an essay-type answer. You may find it helpful to use Table 4.4 as a guide when checking your own work. After such self-assessment you may be able to improve your work.

Improve your writing

An essay, from the French word *essayer* to try, is an attempt to cover a subject in a limited number of words. In an essay, as in any other composition, you also attempt to interest the reader. You attempt to create a short original composition that is complete in itself. An essay has an accepted structure: a beginning (the introductory paragraph); a middle (a few paragraphs arranged in an appropriate sequence); and an end (your conclusion).

Many of the questions set for students, in both coursework and examinations, although they do not include the word essay, require an answer with a similar structure (an introduction, an orderly sequence of paragraphs, and a conclusion), as does a letter and as do most other communications written by professional people as part of their day-to-day work.

Preparing written answers to questions helps you to recognise your strengths and weaknesses. You will learn about the subject at each stage in composition: (a) as you think about the question and consider what could be included; (b) as you gather information and ideas; (c) as you select and arrange your material when preparing a topic outline; (d) as you write; and (e) as you check and, if necessary, revise your work. All the time spent on these different activities is time for thought. It is time well spent, because when your composition is complete your understanding of the subject will have been improved.

Always work to a topic outline as you write

If you have a choice of title, choose a subject that interests you – one you already know something about – or find out about the subject before you write – so that you can select, arrange, and maintain control of your material. As you think about the question set or the title of your composition, use one sheet of paper or your computer screen for rough work, and reconsider these first thoughts later when you are ready to make them into a topic outline (see pages 34–6). Organise your work on each composition over the time available for it, so that you always have time for thinking and planning before you write.

Teachers of all subjects can help their students by asking for a topic outline to be handed in with each assignment. Students should then learn from their teachers' comments, corrections and suggestions, and should ask about anything that they do not understand or that they wish to discuss.

For practice in preparing a written answer in about 30 minutes (as they will have to do in examinations), in a course on communication skills students may be asked to answer a question as a class exercise and to submit a topic outline with their answer at the end of the class.

Learn from successful writers

Learn to improve your writing by studying the techniques of successful writers. Consider, for example, the purpose and scope of leading articles in quality newspapers, and of articles that interest you in magazines relevant to the subjects you are studying.

Study each article carefully. What is it about the title that captured your interest? Does the first sentence make you want to read more?

Reconstruct the author's topic outline by picking out the topic for each paragraph. Is each topic relevant to the title? Are the paragraphs in an appropriate order? How effectively does the last sentence of each paragraph serve as a link with the first sentence of the next? Does the last paragraph provide an effective conclusion? Are the author's arguments convincing? Is the article biased? Is anything omitted that you feel should have been included? Have all your questions been answered?

As a class exercise, a tutor may photocopy an article, cut out the paragraphs, and paste them on to separate sheets so that it is not possible to see the order in which they were arranged by the author. Alternatively, one student can do this, to provide a subject for a meeting of a discussion group. Then all students in the class or group can be asked to pick out the topic sentence for each paragraph, and arrange the paragraphs in what they consider the most appropriate order – before looking to see how the author arranged them.

Discuss your written work with other students

When assessors return your written work consider each of their comments and suggestions carefully. You will be pleased when the only comment is the one word 'Good' and when the mark is good. But you can learn most, whatever the mark, from those assessors who indicate clearly what is good and where there is room for improvement, and suggest how your work could be improved.

Reading an essay to other students, as a small group in a tutorial, can provide a basis for discussion. Sharing ideas on presentation, or topics for paragraphs, or points of detail, may help all members of the group. They learn more about their subject and about the art of composition.

The following are faults commonly encountered in the written work of students. You can help yourself by checking each of your coursework assignments yourself, before handing it in to be marked, to ensure that it has none of these faults.

Lack of planning

As a result of insufficient thought and planning, many students present information and ideas in an ineffective order, or do not make it easy for the assessor's thoughts to move smoothly from the topic of each paragraph to that of the next. Lack of planning is also indicated when information on one topic, which should be brought together in one paragraph, is included in different parts of a composition. This confuses the reader (assessor) and makes marking unnecessarily difficult.

Failure to answer the question

Some students answer the question that they would have liked (especially in examinations when they may be ready with a prepared answer) instead of answering the question set. This is the result of lack of attention to the precise wording of the question, of lack of planning, or of wishful thinking.

Lack of balance

An unbalanced answer, with too much attention paid to some aspects of the question and not enough to others, or with parts of the question ignored, may result from lack of planning or lack of knowledge. Whatever the reason, it is difficult to mark.

All students should appreciate that, to be fair to everyone answering any question, teachers and examiners use a marking scheme in which a fixed number of marks is allocated to each aspect of an answer. In coursework and examinations you would like to score high marks, and should try to give a complete answer to each part of any question. Remember that an assessor cannot give more marks than are available in the marking scheme for any part of the question that receives more attention than is necessary, cannot give all the marks available for the parts that receive less attention than is necessary, and can give no marks for the parts that are ignored.

Failure to capture and hold the reader's interest

To interest the lecturer whose lectures you have been attending, who set the question you are answering as part of your coursework, your answer must be more than a summary of this lecturer's own lecture notes. At least you must include only relevant material from the lectures, arranged in an appropriate order and as an answer to the question set. But, if you can, provide evidence of your own thinking. For example, integrate knowledge gained from all relevant lectures, from your background reading, and from your own observations (for example in field and laboratory studies), as appropriate. See also chapter 8, *Helping your readers*.

Pomposity and verbosity

A common fault in the writing of students, and others, is the use of a long word when a shorter word would serve the purpose better, or of more words than are needed to convey the intended meaning precisely. Anyone preferring long words to more appropriate shorter words may seem pompous, and students who pad their writing with superfluous words are likely both to obscure their meaning and give the impression that they are simply trying to make a little knowledge go a long way – perhaps in the belief that marks are given according to the number of words used or the number of sheets of paper filled.

Lack of care

Many mistakes result from a failure to check the composition. As a result, some sentences do not make sense, others are ambiguous, and slips of the pen go uncorrected.

Benefit from your assessors' criticisms

In coursework and examinations you are usually trying to *explain* something *clearly* and *simply*. Remember that marks are given for *balance* (paying sufficient attention to each part of the question), for *accuracy* and *completeness*, and for the *orderly* presentation of relevant material: that is to say, for content and presentation – which indicate your knowledge and understanding.

When assessed coursework is returned to you, the mark awarded is of immediate interest as an indication of how close your work has come to the standard expected. But you also need to know what was good about your answer, whether it included any mistakes or misunderstandings, and whether or not the assessor has any suggestions that will help you to improve your written work. Consider every comment, correction or suggestion very carefully to see how you can benefit from each assessor's advice. Such constructive criticism will probably be the only instruction on the art of writing you receive from most academics, and it is important because it is specific to your own work – whereas a book for all students can give only general advice.

Because recognising what is good in the work of other students and where there is room for improvement will help you to improve your own compositions, you will also find it useful to look critically at the written work of your friends – and to discuss with them any comments and suggestions made by the assessors who marked their work. Recognising faults in

Table 4.5 How to prepare a handwritten composition in coursework*

Think	1	Consider the title.
	2	Define the purpose and scope of your composition.
	3	Decide who your readers are, and what they need to know. You will usually be writing for one assessor, whose requirements should be clear from the question set.
	4	Allocate your time to thinking, planning, writing and checking.
	5	Make notes of relevant information and ideas.
Plan	6	Prepare a topic outline.
	7	Underline the points that require most emphasis.
	8	Decide on an effective beginning.
	9	Number the topics in an appropriate order.
	10	Decide on an effective conclusion.
Write	11	Use wide-lined A4 paper with a 25 mm ruled margin, to leave yourself enough space for corrections or additions between the lines.
	12	Ensure you will be free from interruptions.
	13	Write your name, the title (usually the question set) and the date.
	14	Use your topic outline as a guide, so that you can keep to the point and keep going until your composition is complete – expressing your thoughts as clearly and simply as you can.
Check	15	Check that every word is legible, that everything is relevant, and that nothing is repeated unintentionally; make any corrections or other improvements; and check that all the points you intended to emphasise are clearly made.
	16	If possible, put your composition on one side for a few days and then look at it afresh. Try to assess your work. Revise it if necessary. Keep a copy.

Note
* When word processing a document you will probably start with a handwritten first draft, unless you can touch type (see chapter 13, *Your computer as an aid to writing*).

the writing of others should help you to avoid making similar mistakes in your own writing – and so to improve your own written work.

Prepare every composition in four stages

If you follow the basic advice given in this chapter (see Table 4.5), which applies to all your writing as a student and in any profession based on your studies, whether you are using a pen or a word processor, you should find that with practice your writing continues to improve.

5 Thoughts into words

The popularity of crossword puzzles and other word games is an indication of the fun to be had from words; as is the fact that many jokes are a play on words. Our interest in the meaning of words, and our pleasure in using words, is not surprising – because each time we speak we are trying to put our thoughts into words. Indeed, the use of words is even more fundamental than this. Without words we cannot think; and we are limited in our ability to think by the number of words at our command. As we enlarge our vocabulary, and learn to construct effective sentences and paragraphs, we improve our ability to think and to express our thoughts and feelings.

We write so that we can tell others what we think, but if we use words incorrectly, or choose words our readers do not understand, we shall be misunderstood. So we must think about words, choose words we expect our readers to know, and use them correctly in carefully constructed sentences.

Vocabulary

One of the delights of English is its rich vocabulary. No two words are identical in meaning, and the choice of one word where another would make more sense does not help readers. When *The Times* newspaper reported that it was paying Rudyard Kipling by the word for an article, a student sent him some money and asked for one of his best words. Kipling replied, 'Thanks'.

The right word does not always come so readily to mind, and people who have too few words at their command may fall back on hackneyed phrases or clichés, such as: *first and foremost; in this day and age; it goes without saying; in well-informed circles; at the right psychological moment; feel compelled to admit; to all intents and purposes; with no shadow of doubt; in any shape or form;* and *last but not least, conspicuous by its absence.* Instead, they should take trouble to find the word or words which express their meaning precisely.

In Patrick Dennis' *Auntie Mame* (1955), Mame considered a rich vocabulary the true hallmark of every intellectual person. To encourage her young nephew to take an interest in words she gave him a pad and pencil, and asked him to write down any word that he didn't understand so that she could tell him its meaning.

> 'Then you memorise it and soon you'll have a decent vocabulary. Oh, the adventure', she cried ecstatically, 'of moulding a little new life!' She made another sweeping gesture that somehow went wrong because she knocked over the coffee pot and I immediately wrote down six new words which Auntie Mame said to scratch out and forget about.

You may use words that you understand, and that your readers understand, yet still write sentences that are difficult to read. In learning your own language you were probably encouraged to develop your ability to use long words, write complex sentences, exercise your imagination, and include adjectives, metaphors and similes to make your descriptions more vivid and colourful. Perhaps this is why some people seem to think that such writing is necessary to demonstrate their cleverness to the world.

On the contrary, in most scholarly writing you should be trying to convey your meaning as clearly and simply as you can. Do not write long involved sentences, with many long words. And never use long words simply for effect. Prefer a short word to a long one (see Table 5.1), unless the longer word will serve your purpose better; and prefer a single word to a phrase if brevity makes for clarity (see Table 6.4).

In Charles Dickens' novel *David Copperfield* (1850), Mr Micawber had the habit of using long words to impress and then providing a translation so that he could be understood.

> 'Under the impression', said Mr Micawber, 'that your peregrinations in this metropolis have not as yet been extensive, and that you might have some difficulty in penetrating the arcana of the Modern Babylon in the direction of the City Road – in short,' said Mr Micawber in another burst of confidence, 'that you might lose yourself . . .'

Some people like fashionable words, such as confrontational, currently, deprived, dialogue, environment, escalation, facility, guesstimate, hopefully, importantly, informed, integrated, interface, meaningful, nice, non-event, obscene, ongoing, overall, paradigm, relevant, situation, supportive, strategy, syndrome, traumatic, underprivileged, within, workshop. The rapid dating of fashionable words and phrases is particularly noticeable

Table 5.1 Prefer a short word to a long word if the short word is more appropriate

Instead of this	Prefer this	Instead of this	Prefer this
absolutely	yes	hypothesise	suggest
accomplish	do	importantly	important
adequate	enough	indication	sign
additional	extra	individual	person
anticipate	expect	individuals	people
application	use	initiate	start
approximately	about	manufacture	make
assistance	help	modification	change
commence	begin	permit	let
concerning	about	possess	have
consequently	so	practically	nearly
considerable	much	presently	soon[b]
currently[a]	now[a]	proceed	go
demonstrate	show	regarding	about
discontinue	stop	represents	is
donate	give	streamlined	shortened
encounter	meet	subsequently	later[b]
endeavour	try	sufficient	enough
excepting	except	terminate	end
fabricate	build	transpire	happen
firstly	first	upon	on
forward	send	utilise (or utilisation)	use
guidelines	guidance	virtually	almost
humans (or human beings)	people	within	in

Notes
a But omit if superfluous (see Table 5.4).
b Be precise if you can: say when.

with euphemisms. For example, people once known as *the poor*, have been described as *needy*, then *deprived*, then *disadvantaged*, then *underprivileged* (less privileged than the few who are privileged). The euphemisms get longer but the poor people remain poor.

Fashionable words may lose their impact through overuse. They may be devalued if they are used even when other words would be more appropriate. Discerning writers may then avoid such words, with the result that they may be words to avoid even after they have gone out of fashion.

When people think something is too technical for them, it may be that the writing is at fault. Unfortunately, some writers seem to think scholarly writing must be hard reading, and that they impress people by adopting a pompous style. But their studied avoidance of short words is not likely to impress, and is very likely to annoy, confuse or amuse. This anonymous nursery rhyme pokes fun at grandiloquence:

Scintillate, scintillate, globule aurific,
Fain would I fathom thy nature specific,
Loftily poised in the ether capacious,
Strongly resembling a gem carbonaceous.

You know the rhyme? Perhaps you have heard something like it. People do prefer short words. That is why most people call their telephone a phone, refer to their photographs as photos, and shorten the term violoncello to cello.

The meaning of words

Keep a good dictionary to hand, on your bookshelf or in your desk drawer, as a guide to the correct spelling and pronunciation of each word listed, its origin, its current status in the language, and its several meanings (see *References*, page 209).

A dictionary provides excellent reading. As Eric Partridge (1949) pointed out in his *English: A Course for Human Beings*, the stories in a dictionary are short but each time you read one you learn something:

> you understand the word the next time you see it in print or hear it spoken – and you can use it . . . without your companions glancing at one another in that odd way which is so much more disconcerting than outright laughter.

Some people write words in quotation marks (in 'quotes': inverted commas) to indicate that they are not quite the right words, or that they are not using them in the usual sense, or that they imply more than they are prepared to state clearly. But using quotation marks in this way could confuse some readers. So, to ensure clarity, it is best to choose words that convey your meaning precisely.

Some words that many people confuse

It is necessary to have a good vocabulary not only so that you can express your own thoughts clearly and understand other people when they use words correctly but also to help you understand what others probably mean when they use words incorrectly. So, consult a dictionary before using any word, if you are unsure of its meaning. Check, for example, that when expressing yourself you do not confuse the following words.

Accept (receive) with *except* (not including).

Advice (counsel, a noun) with *advise* (to give advice).

Advise (to give advice) with *inform* (tell).

Affect (to alter or influence) with *effect* (a verb meaning to bring about or a noun meaning a result).

Aggravate (make worse) with *annoy* (vex) or *irritate* (cause irritation).

Alternate (to perform by turns) with *alternately* (first one thing then an alternative, repeatedly, as with a light flashing on and off), and *alternatively* (referring to one thing as an alternative to another).

Alternative (one of two possibilities) with a *choice* or *option* (one of any number of possibilities).

Amount (mass or volume of something measured) with *number* (of things counted).

Any one and *every one* (numbers) with *anyone* (anybody) and *everyone* (everybody).

Appraise (value or judge) with *apprise* (inform).

Born (given birth to) with *borne* (carried, endured, borne in mind, borne out by).

Complement (a verb meaning to add to or to make complete, or a noun meaning the full number or quantity) with *compliment* (a verb meaning to congratulate, or a noun meaning a word or words of praise).

Complementary (adding to) with *complimentary* (without charge or in praise of).

Continual (repeatedly) with *continuous* (non-stop).

Council (a committee) with *counsel* (advice, an advisor, or to advise).

Data (Latin *dare*, to give) with *results* (which are derived from data by deduction, calculation or processing). Data (sing. *datum*) are things given, facts of any kind, observations recorded as numbers (numerical data) or using words. It is incorrect, therefore, to speak of raw data, but correct to refer to original observations as original data.

Defective (not working) with *deficient* (lacking some essential).

Dependant (one who is dependent) with *dependent* (relying on).

Deprecate (disapprove) with *depreciate* (decrease in value).

Discreet (prudent, wary) with *discrete* (separate, distinct).

Disinterested (impartial) with *uninterested* (not interested).

Each other (which refers to two) with *one another* (referring to more than two).

Enquire (ask) with *inquire* (investigate), and an *enquiry* (a question) with an *inquiry* (an investigation).

Farther (more distant) with *further* (additional).

Fewer (a smaller number of) with *less* (smaller in mass or volume): for example, it is possible to have fewer people, but not to have less people.

Forego (go before) with *forgo* (go without).

Fortunate (lucky or prosperous) with *fortuitous* (by chance).

Historic (having a memorable place in history) with *historical* (in the past).

Homogeneous (similar in composition throughout) with *homogenous* (similar as a result of genetic relationship).

Imply with *infer*. A speaker or writer may imply (hint at) more than is stated explicitly; and from this a listener or reader may infer (guess at or understand) the intended message.

Initiate (begin something) with *instigate* (persuade someone else to do something).

Its (possessive, indicating that something belongs to someone or is part of something) with *it's* (colloquial, a contraction meaning either it is or it has).

Licence (permission, a permit, abuse of freedom) with *license* (to authorise or to grant a permit).

Meter (a measuring instrument) with *metre* (1000 mm).

Method (how to perform a task) with *methodology* (the study of method).

Of course (certainly) with *off course* (not on course).

Oral (spoken, pertaining to the mouth) with *verbal* (using words – in singing, speaking or writing).

Practicable (feasible, something that could be done) with *practical* (not theoretical). Something may be considered impracticable because it is not considered cost effective, but to say that something is not a practical proposition means that it could not be done.

Practice (a noun meaning the way things are usually done, or a business) with *practise* (a verb meaning to do habitually, to train, or to exercise a profession).

Principal (first in rank, main, a capital sum) with *principle* (a fundamental truth, a rule of conduct one is unlikely to break – as a matter of principle).

Results (obtained by analysing data) with *data* (data: see also page 55).

Review (a survey) with *revue* (an entertainment).

Since (from that time) with *because* (for this reason).

Stationary (not moving) with *stationery* (writing paper).

Their (indicating possession, as in their house, their interests) with *there* (used with the verb to be, as in *there is*, *there are*, *there was*, *there were*; and to indicate a place, as in over *there*).

To (as in to go) with *too* (as in too much).

True (correct, real, right) with *valid* (sound).

Venal (a person who may be bought) with *venial* (pardonable).

Verbal (using words) with *oral* (spoken). In speaking face to face we use facial expressions and other body language (non-verbal communication) as well as words, whereas in writing we have to rely on words alone.

Whose (possessive, as in Whose pen is this?) with *Who's* (colloquial, meaning who is, as in Who's coming? or who has, as in Who's been?)

Within (enclosed by) with *in* (inside). Many people use the word within when the word in would serve their purpose better: for such people, apparently, the word in is 'out'. Something may be within these walls or within the bounds of possibility, but unless some such limits are intended the word in should be preferred.

Your (possessive) with *you're* (colloquial, meaning you are).

Some other words that are commonly confused are listed on page 67, for consideration but without explanation.

Most words have more than one meaning, and a word may take on a new meaning when people need to convey a new idea (or a new word may be invented). An old word may continue to be used with its new meaning, in a new context, long after it has gone out of use in its original context. The word broadcast, for example, which once referred only to the spreading of grain, was later used for the spreading of words: first by wireless (a new word at the time), then by radio (another new word), and then for the spreading of words and pictures in television (an even newer word).

Some words that many people misuse

The meaning of a word may change so much, as a result of its misuse, that it no longer conveys meaning precisely. Consider, for example, the following words.

Approximate(ly) means very close(ly) and should not be used when *about* or *roughly* would be more appropriate.

Current(ly) means now, and the shorter word should be preferred (see Table 5.1), but in most sentences the word currently is superfluous (see Tautology, Table 5.4). For example, *We are currently* . . . means *We are* . . . (and *We are currently in the process of* . . . also means *We are* . . .).

A *democracy* is a state practising government by the people, but this word has been abused by dictators of countries in which the citizens have no political rights.

Integral. An integer is a whole number or a thing complete in itself. Do not write an integral part (meaning a whole part, not a part of a part) if you simply mean a part.

Literally is a word that should be used rarely, if at all, by most writers. It means actually (a word that is usually superfluous, see Table 5.3), or without exaggeration, yet is commonly used in an attempt to affirm the truth of an exaggeration. For example: 'My eyes were literally glued to the television screen'.

Majority (the greater number) does not mean *most* (nearly all). In an election, for example, a person may be elected with a majority of one. If you read that 'the majority of writers use word processors', does this mean that nearly all writers use them? Does anyone know what proportion of writers use them? Would it be better to say simply that many writers use them? What is the difference, quantitatively, between the majority and the vast majority? Clearly, the word majority is used by

Table 5.2 The word *often* misused

Incorrect*	Correct
People *often* may not know the meaning of words which seem obvious to you	*Some* people may not understand words that you know well.
One reason why reports are *often* not well written is . . .	One reason *many* reports are badly written is . . .
The longest words we use are *often* abstract nouns.	*Many* writers use abstract nouns when shorter concrete nouns would serve their purpose better.
You may have learnt the dangerous lesson complicated language *often* impresses people.	You may have learnt that *many* people are impressed by . . .
When we point out illiterate mistakes we are *often* aggressively instructed to . . .	When we point out the mistakes of illiterates, *many* instruct us to . . .

Note
* From books on the English language

some writers – when they are unable to be precise – as a substitute for evidence (see *Use numbers when you can be precise*, page 85).

Often. 'People who eat mushrooms often die' (but people who do not eat mushrooms die only once!). 'I often eat fish on Friday' (whereas most people, if they eat fish on Friday, do so only once). Do not write often if you mean *some*, *many* or *most* (see Table 5.2).

Parameters (Greek *para*: about, *metron*: measure) are characteristics of a population (estimates of which, based on samples, are called statistics). For example, the sample mean is an estimator of the population mean – which it is not usually possible or practicable to measure. Prefer *boundary* (perimeter), or *limit*, if one of these words conveys your meaning.

Percentage. If you cannot be precise, prefer many to a large percentage of . . ., and few to a small percentage of . . . That is to say, do not use the word percentage unless you can say what percentage.

Progress means a move forward, an improvement, a change for the better, but the word is misused for change of any kind. Indeed, the most outrageous suggestion may seem to acquire a certain respectability if someone calls it an improvement or progress. As Herbert Mundin said in 1926, in his monologue about London's last cabby (cabman):

> It does not always happen
> That change is for the good.
> More often it's the opposite
> I find.

Refute should be used in the sense of proving falsity or error. It is not a synonym for *deny* (declare false) or *repudiate* (reject or disavow).

Significant is a statistical term with a precise meaning. Care is needed when using it in other contexts if readers are to know whether or not you mean statistically significant.

Since is a word that can confuse readers, or get in the way of understanding at first reading, if used when the meaning intended is *as* or *because*. It is best to use since only when referring to a period of time.

Sophisticated (Greek *sophistes*: wise man, wizard) was for long an uncomplimentary word implying sophistry or artfulness, but it has also been used to mean complicated or to imply that a new instrument is in some way better than an earlier model. In this context it is an imprecise word that conveys no information and is perhaps now out of fashion.

Statistics are numerical data systematically collected, and the results of the analysis of such data.

Viable means having the capacity to live but some people say *not viable* in contexts when they mean *impracticable, too expensive* or *will not work*.

Vital means essential to life and it is best not to use this word in other contexts.

While means at the same time (as in 'Nero fiddled while Rome burned'). So do not write while if you mean *and* (as in 'I prefer squash while you prefer tennis') or if you mean *but* (as in 'On Saturday I work while on Sunday I rest'); and do not write while or whilst if you mean *although*.

Try not to use two words if only one is needed. In particular, do not qualify words that have only one meaning (see Table 5.3). *Unique*, for example, means the only one of its kind. So do not write *quite unique*: this is an unnecessary qualification of the word unique; and perhaps those who write *almost unique* mean rare. Similarly, *facts* are things known to be true. So it is wrong to refer to *the fact that* energy may be involved, or to write that the

Table 5.3 The incorrect qualification of words

Incorrect	Correct
they really are	they are
deliberately avoided	avoided
blue in colour	blue
an essential condition	a condition
conical in shape	conical
under active consideration	being considered
definitely (or quite) correct	correct
really dangerous	dangerous
not really dangerous	safe?
a definite decision	a decision
a categorical denial	a denial
absolutely essential	essential
hard evidence	evidence
in actual fact	in fact
they are in fact	they are
few in number	few
hilly in character	hilly
literally impermeable	impermeable
realistic justification	justification
the smallest possible minimum	the minimum
really (or very) necessary	necessary
wholly new	new
the actual number	the number
quite obvious	obvious
absolutely perfect	perfect
real pleasure	pleasure
very real problems	problems
conclusive proof	proof
refer back	refer or refer again
positively rejected	rejected
very relevant	relevant
seasonal in occurrence	seasonal
small in size	small
genuinely sorry	sorry
streamlined in appearance	streamlined
stunted in growth	stunted
completely surrounded	surrounded
very true	true
not actually true	untrue
quite unique	unique

evidence points to the fact, or to suggest that someone has *got the facts wrong*, and to speak of the *actual facts* is to say the same thing twice (see Table 5.4)

Many people write *it comprises of* when they should write either *it comprises* or *it consists of*. Other words and the prepositions that should follow them, according to accepted usage, are: absolve from, abstain from,

Table 5.4 Tautology: saying the same thing twice using different words

Do not write this	Write this
in the field of agriculture	in agriculture
or, alternatively, . . .	alternatively, . . .
are currently	are
are currently in the process of	are
ask the question whether	ask whether
the reason for this is because	because
an extra added bonus	a bonus
but . . . however	but or however
in the rural countryside	in the countryside
disappear from sight	disappear
enclosed with this letter	enclosed
give positive encouragement	encourage
eradicate completely	eradicate
a specific example	an example
in actual fact	in fact
equally as good	equally good/as good
group together	group
two equal halves	halves
a tentative hypothesis	a hypothesis
linked together	linked
a temporary loan	a loan
I may possibly . . .	I may . . .
every individual one	every one
my own personal opinion	my opinion
an integral part	a part
percolate down	percolate
each individual person	each person
advance planning	planning
postpone to a later date	postpone
related to each other	related
will not recur again	will not recur
continue to remain	remain
reverted back to woodland again	reverted to woodland
one after another in succession	in succession
a tentative suggestion	a suggestion
superimposed over each other	superimposed
symptoms indicative of	symptoms
from now on through to the end of	until the end of
on the same day that	on the day that
still in use today	still used
different varieties	varieties
on pages 1–4 inclusive	on pages 1–4
an assassination attempt on the life of	an assassination attempt on *or* an attempt on the life of

accompanied by, in accordance with, amenable to, collaborate with, compatible with, confirm in, conform to, connive at, consequent upon, correspond to (a thing), correspond with (a person), concur in (an opinion), concur with (a person), defer to, deficient in, impervious to, indifferent to, indicative of, preferable to, preoccupied with, refrain from, responsible for (an action), responsible to (a person) and substitute for (but replace by).

The words of your subject

As you study a subject you acquire a vocabulary of specialist terms that make for easy communication with other people studying the same subject, but are a barrier to communication between specialists and non-specialists (and also between people specialising in different subjects, see Figure 5.1). For example, the following words are used by people with different interests.

Chemistry: asymmetry, bond, compound, desiccate, filtrate, law, organic, soluble

Ecology: alpine, biome, community, diurnal, epiphyte, habitat, predator, succession

English language: antonym, clause, consonant, etymology, interjection, preposition

English literature: descriptive, essay, lyric, metre, narrative, novel, play, rhyme

Golf: birdie, bogey, divot, fairway, green, hook, lie, links, play, putt, rough, tee

Government: act, constitution, democracy, fascist, law, oligarchy, politics, rule

History: accession, dynasty, empire, rule, historic, historical, nation, succession

Music: arpeggio, brass, concerto, melody, note, octave, rock, syncopation

To make it easier for learners to acquire the additional vocabulary needed when studying a new subject, authors of textbooks should write as simply and clearly as they can; and specialists who hope to interest non-specialists should explain any essential technical terms the first time they use them in any composition.

Well . . . er . . . this is it.

Figure 5.1 Every subject (art, craft, science, or sport) has its own specialist or technical terms that may not be understood by non-specialists. In your writing, use words you expect your readers to understand

When you write a technical term, you make two assumptions that may not be justified: you assume that the reader (a) is familiar with the concept, and (b) will recognise the concept by its technical name. Before using any technical term, therefore, consider whether or not it will help your readers. Do not use specialist terms in an attempt to impress non-specialist readers. For non-specialist readers, use an everyday word or phrase if you can. If the technical term is essential provide a concise definition or an illustration (for example, a line drawing with labels to make clear the names of the parts illustrated, as in Figure 7.1).

However, as a student you should appreciate the value of the specialist words of your subject, and should show your knowledge and understanding by using them correctly in appropriate contexts. Unless you understand them and can define them, you will be handicapped in all your studies. See *Prepare definitions*, page 68.

For example, until you are certain of the meaning of every word used in any question you cannot begin to plan a complete and correct answer. Then in your answer, assessors and examiners will expect you to use these words in appropriate contexts, to show that you understand them, to define them if necessary, and to spell them correctly.

The candidate who spelt satellite in eight ways in one answer – even though the correct spelling was given in the question – did not impress the examiner. Nor did the students of English literature who could not spell correctly the names of characters in their set books, or the students of European history who could not spell the names Disraeli, Victor Emmanuel, Napoleon and Peel. Correct spelling is important (see chapter 15, *Spelling check*).

Abbreviations, contractions and acronyms

The use of abbreviations, contractions and acronyms saves space. They are especially useful in tables, in column headings. However, in scholarly writing, prefer complete words that you feel confident your readers will understand.

Misunderstandings are possible even when readers recognise an abbreviation. One problem is that the abbreviation may have more than one meaning, even in one language: for example, in English adv. = advent, adverb, advertisement; and d. = daughter, day, deceased, dollar, dose, penny (a pre-decimal coin). Another problem is that many dictionaries of abbreviations are hastily compiled and inaccurate, and are no sooner published than they are out of date (Potter, 1966). So a puzzled reader who troubled to consult a dictionary of abbreviations might not discover which if any of the meanings listed the writer intended.

In writing English, avoid phrases from other languages, and abbreviations of such phrases. For example, avoid the abbreviations *loc. cit.* (in the place cited), *op. cit.* (in the work cited) and *ibid.* (in the same work) which some readers might not understand, and which even if understood can (like the words former and latter) contribute to ambiguity. Except in your own note-taking, write that is (not i.e. = *id est*), and for example (not e.g. = *exempli gratia*), because even these commonly used abbreviations are misused, and are therefore misunderstood, by some British people who have passed their school-leaving examinations. For the same reason, write namely (not *viz.*), and as written (not *sic.* = *sicut*, just as), and prefer about to *circa*, *ca.*, or *c.* And, because the abbreviation etc. (*et cetera*: and other things) used at the end of a list tells readers only that the list is incomplete, it is better to write the words for example or including immediately before the list. Note the use of the full stop in this paragraph to indicate an abbreviation.

Note that letters indicating qualifications (for example, BA, BSc, PhD) and contractions, which include the final letter of a word (for example Mr and Dr), are not punctuated (nos., for numbers, is an exception). Note also that acronyms, for example, ISO, UNESCO and WHO (comprising the initial letters of the International Standards Organisation, the United Nations Educational, Scientific and Cultural Organisation, and the World Health Organisation) are not punctuated. And remember: (a) that a full stop should not be placed after a symbol for an SI unit of measurement (see Table 7.1); and (b) that an s should not be added to an abbreviation, contraction or symbol in forming the plural. Exceptions to this last rule are the contractions chs for chapters, nos. for numbers, vols for volumes, and figs for figures in the sense of illustrations.

In your writing try to convey your meaning without using abbreviations, contractions and acronyms, but if any are essential remember to explain each one the first time you use it in any composition (for example, in parenthesis in the text or in a footnote to a table) if its meaning may not be clear to some of your readers.

Improve your writing

1   Prefer a short word to a long word unless the long word will serve your purpose better (see Table 5.1).
2   Make sure that you understand the meaning of the words you use, so that you can use them correctly (see Tables 5.2 to 5.4).
3   Do not write words in inverted commas ('quotes') to signpost that you are not using them in the accepted sense, or that you do not really mean what you say. Instead, choose words that convey your meaning precisely.
4   Show your understanding of the words you use by using them correctly, in appropriate contexts, in properly constructed sentences.
5   Avoid abbreviations, contractions and acronyms if you can.

Choose words with care

Cover Table 5.1 with a sheet of paper, then uncover column 1 and suggest a shorter word that you could use instead of each of the words listed, before you look at column 2; then consider each of the words listed in column 3 before you look at column 4.

Cover Table 5.2 with a sheet of paper, then uncover column 1 and suggest how the same meaning should be conveyed in fewer words.

Cover Table 5.3 with a sheet of paper, then uncover column 1 and, for each entry, suggest which word or words should be deleted.

Use your dictionary

Consult your dictionary whenever you come across a word that you do not understand. You will satisfy your curiosity, increase the number of words at your command, and find this a lifelong source of enlightenment and pleasure.

Consult your dictionary now if you need help in distinguishing between: *admitted* and *said*, *adverse* and *averse*, *affectation* and *affection*, *alibi* and *excuse*, *all together* and *altogether*, *allude* and *refer*, *allusion* and *illusion*, *always* and *everywhere*, *among* and *between*, *anticipate* and *expect*, *appreciate* and *understand*, *beside* and *besides*, *biannual* and *biennial*, *breath* and *breathe*, *canon* and *cannon*, *canvas* and *canvass*, *centre* and *middle*, *centred on* and *around* or *close to* (not *centred around*), *childish* and *childlike*, *circle* and *disc*, *degree* and *extent*, *device* and *devise*, *economic* and *economical*, *effective* and *efficient*, *elicit* and *illicit*, *especially* and *specially*, *exceedingly* and *excessively*, *except* and *unless*, *explicit* and *implicit*, *formally* and *formerly*, *generally* and *usually*, *if* and *although*, *inform* and *influence*, *ingenious* and *ingenuous*, *interfere* and *intervene*, *lengthy* and *long*, *lightening* and *lightning*, *limited* and *few* (*small*, *slight* or *narrow*), *loose* and *lose*, *luxuriant* and *luxurious*, *marshal* and *martial*, *masterful* and *masterly*, *minor* and *little*, *moral* and *morale*, *myself* and *me*, *natural* and *normal*, *notable* and *noticeable*, *optimistic* and *hopeful*, *optimum* and *highest*, *percentage* and *some*, *populace* and *populous*, *practically* and *almost*, *precede* and *proceed*, *prescribe* and *proscribe*, *quite* and *entirely* (or *rather*), *recourse* and *resource*, *reverend* and *reverent*, *same* and *identical* (or *similar*), *seasonable* and *seasonal*, *sceptic* and *septic*, *singular* and *notable* or *unique*, *some times* and *sometimes*, *superior to* and *better than*, *suspect* and *surmise*, *transpire* and *happen*, *urban* and *urbane*, *view* and *opinion*, *virtually* and *almost*, *volume* and *amount*, *wastage* and *waste*, *weather* and *climate*.

Understand the words used in questions

Consider carefully and make sure you understand the precise meaning of each of the following words used in the questions set in coursework, tests and examinations: account, analyse, argue, comment, compare, consider, define, describe, discuss, essay, evaluate, evidence, explain, illustrate, list, opinion, outline, review, state, summarise.

Many students miss opportunities to score marks, when they could prepare good answers to the questions set, because they do not consider carefully the meaning of each word in any question before planning their answer, when preparing their topic outline, and before starting to write (see *Analyse the question*, page 32).

Make sure you understand what is required, then answer the question set. Respond to its precise wording. You may be instructed to answer *in a few words*, or *in your own words*, or *in full detail*. You may be asked *to assess the relative importance of* . . . or *to suggest to what extent* . . . or *to state how far* . . . If asked to name *one* . . . do not name two, or if asked to give *one* example of . . . do not give two. You will be given little credit for writing everything you can remember from your revision notes on the subject of a question, or for writing all you know about any subject, if what you write is not an answer to the question.

Prepare definitions

You may know how to use a word in an appropriate context and yet have difficulty in defining it precisely. This is why in a test you may be asked to define a word; and in an examination you may need to include definitions in your answers to some questions to make clear your understanding.

When you have to define a word, note the points that must be included (as you would when preparing a topic outline for a longer composition). Then write your definition.

In any definition, start with the general and proceed to the particular. That is to say, state the general class to which the thing to be defined belongs (for example, a verb is a word) and then the features peculiar to the thing defined (it is a word that indicates action). Your definition must be as simple as possible but it must apply to all instances of the thing defined (all verbs in this example) and to no others (no other kinds of words). Your definition may be followed by an example. See Table 14.1.

6 Using words

Words in context

In a dictionary, each word is first explained and then used in appropriate contexts to make its several meanings clear. For words do not stand alone: each word gives meaning to and takes meaning from the sentence, so that there is more to the whole than might be expected from its parts. The words in a sentence should tie each other down so that, with necessary punctuation marks, the sentence as a whole has only one meaning.

Position your words with care

The position of a word in a sentence should reflect the emphasis you wish to put upon it. An important word may, for example, come near the beginning or near the end of a sentence, and in either position it may help to link the ideas expressed in successive sentences. The position of a word in a sentence can also transform the meaning of the sentence.

For example, the word *only* is well known for the trouble it can cause when out of place (see Table 6.1). Consider also the meaning of each of the following sentences. 'I *only* eat fish on Fridays.' 'I eat *only* fish on Fridays.' 'I eat fish *only* on Fridays.' 'I eat fish on Fridays *only*.' 'I don't eat meat on Fridays.' The meaning intended in the first of these sentences is probably that conveyed by the last (which does not include the word only). In conversation most people would perhaps take this meaning, not from what was said but from the context, the intonation and the accompanying facial expression. When reading they can take the meaning only from what is written.

Fowler (1968) considers that writers should not be forced to spend time considering which part of the sentence is qualified by the word only, yet advises that it is bad to misplace this word when in the wrong place it would spoil or obscure the meaning.

Table 6.1 Examples of the word *only* out of place

Extracts from books	Meaning intended
In this book those points of grammar only are discussed which will help you to ensure accuracy.	In this book only those points of grammar that will help you to ensure accuracy are discussed.
The words no doubt should only be used when the idea of certainty is to be conveyed.	The words no doubt should be used only when the idea of certainty is to be conveyed
I can only write well when I know what I want to say.	I can write well only when I know what I want to say.
It only works well for straightforward pieces of descriptive writing.	It works well only for straightforward descriptive writing.
The chemical was only manufactured in Europe.	The chemical was manufactured only in Europe.
She only made one journey which aroused the interest of detectives.	Only one of her journeys aroused the interest of detectives.
He could only see an expanse of muddy fields and grey sky.	He could see only an expanse of muddy fields and grey sky.

However, it is always worth spending time, when checking your work, in an attempt to ensure that what you write does express precisely what you mean. If any word or punctuation mark is misplaced, the meaning conveyed may not be the meaning you intended. Do not expect your readers to waste their time trying to guess what you probably meant.

Take care when using the pronouns *this*, *that* and *it* (*he* or *she*), *its* (*his* and *hers*); and *one*, *former* and *latter*; and *other* and *another*, or ambiguity may result. For example: 'He gave him his book.' (Whose book?) and 'Elgar played the violin under Dvorak when he was 22.' (Who was 22?). If necessary, repeat a noun to ensure the reader understands your message at first reading.

Repeat a word if necessary

Some people have favourite words and phrases (for example, also, apparently, case, found, incidentally, in fact, perhaps, quite) which they use so often that readers notice the undue repetition. This is because the use of a word twice in a sentence, several times in a paragraph, or many times on one page, can interrupt the smooth flow of language. However, in your writing do not replace the right word by a less apt word just for the sake of what is called elegant variation. Repeat a word if it is the one that best serves your purpose, or, if necessary, for emphasis (see page 104).

Use standard English

In scholarly writing, except when reporting conversation, it is best to use standard language and to avoid colloquial language and slang.

> *Standard English* is language used formally, as in business communications.

> *Colloquial English* is language used informally, as in a letter to a close friend or in conversation. Except when reporting speech, colloquial English should not be used in scholarly writing. In particular do not use such contractions as don't (for do not), it's (for it is or it has), they're (for they are), who's (for who is or who has), and won't (for will not).

> *Slang* is highly colloquial language, including new words or words used in a special sense.

In his *Usage and Abusage: A Guide to Good English*, Eric Partridge (1965) gives, as an example of the difference: man (standard), chap (colloquial); and bloke, bozo, guy and stiff (slang). The words fellow and boy are also standard English.

Avoid ready-made phrases

In scholarly writing, it is also best to avoid clichés (see page 51) and idiomatic expressions (see Table 6.2) in which words have a special meaning that might not be understood by some readers.

In a much-quoted essay on Politics and the English Language, Orwell (1946) wrote:

> As soon as certain topics are raised . . . no one seems able to think in turns of speech that are not hackneyed: prose consists less and less of words chosen for the sake of their meaning, and more and more of phrases tacked together like sections of a prefabricated hen-house.

In using such ready-made phrases, which make less impact than would something new, people deny themselves the simple pleasure of putting their own thoughts into their own words. Instead, try to follow the advice in Jerry Herman's lyric for the 1966 musical *Mame*: always open a new window, open a new door; and travel a new highway, that has never been travelled before.

Table 6.2 Avoid idiomatic expressions

Idiomatic expression	Meaning
break new ground	start something new
explore every avenue	consider all possibilities
in the pipeline	being prepared
it goes without saying	obviously
read between the lines	understand more than is said or written
work against time	try to finish in the time available

Superfluous words

A well-constructed sentence should have neither too many words nor too few: each word should be there for a purpose (see Figure 6.1). Any unnecessary words can only confuse, distract and annoy readers, yet the use of too many words is a more common fault in writing than the use of the wrong word.

Fowler and Fowler (1906) advised anyone wishing to become a good writer to concentrate on being direct, simple, brief, vigorous and lucid. To help in the choice of words, they gave the following rules.

1   Prefer the familiar word to the far-fetched.
2   Prefer concrete nouns (things you can touch and see) to abstract nouns.
3   Prefer the single word to the circumlocution (see Tables 6.3 and 6.4).
4   Prefer the short word to the long (see Table 5.1).
5   Prefer the Saxon word (of German origin) to the Romance word (derived from Latin).

Quiller-Couch (1916), in his lectures on the art of writing, added to this list.

6   Prefer transitive verbs (that strike their object) and use them in the active voice (see Table 6.5).

Quiller-Couch advised anyone who would like to avoid jargon to use abstract nouns sparingly and with care. He listed the words case, character, condition, degree, instance, nature and persuasion as indicators of jargon (for examples, see Tables 4.1, 6.3 and 6.4). Fowler (1968) considered the over-use of abstract nouns to be an indication of cloudy thinking, symptomatic of the disease abstractitis. Of course there is nothing wrong with abstract nouns when they are needed to convey meaning.

Many introductory, connecting, commenting and summarising phrases

'*I cut out only necessary words*'

Figure 6.1 In your writing cut out all unnecessary words

help readers to move smoothly from one paragraph to the next, follow arguments, and confirm that they understand the writer's message. But others in common use should be deleted, because they convey no meaning and do not help readers (see Tables 4.1 and 4.2). If you are in the habit of using such phrases, cut them out and your writing will be more direct, easier to read, and therefore more effective in conveying your meaning.

Circumlocution – verbosity – gobbledegook – surplusage – this habit of excess in the use of words, which makes communication more difficult than necessary, is well established in the speech and writing of many people. As long ago as 1667, in his *History of the Royal Society*, Thomas Sprat wrote that:

> . . . of all the Studies of men, nothing may be sooner obtain'd than this vicious abundance of *Phrase*, this trick of *Metaphors*, this volubility of *Tongue*, which makes so great a noise in the World. But I spend words in vain; for the evil is now so inveterate, that it is hard to know whom

Table 6.3 Circumlocution: the use of many words where fewer would be better[a]

Circumlocution	Better English
a certain *amount* of difficulty	some difficulty
on a dawn to dusk *basis*	from dawn to dusk
We are continuing to review the situation on a daily *basis.*	We review the situation daily.
Such is by no means the *case.*	This is not so.
in the *case* of the first question	in the first question
The standard of English was poor in most *cases.*	The English of most candidates was poor.
a high *degree* of support	strong support
in the school *environment*	in schools
in the *field* of medicine	in medicine
on the educational *front*	in education
at the pre-school *level*	The under-fives
They were poor in the *majority* of *cases.*	Most were poor.
There was a large *measure* of agreement.	Most people agreed.
It was of a controversial *nature*	It was controversial
There is a good *deal* of uncertainty with respect to the overall *position.*	We do not know what is happening.
Few candidates were not in a *position* to offer . . .	Most candidates offered . . .
We are actually in the *process* of	We are . . .
Is this a temporary *situation* or is it permanent?	Is this temporary?
from the *standpoint* of soils	in soils
a more recent *type* of . . .	a more recent . . .
no more than 20 000 to 25 000 words in length	no more than 25 000 words
ten metres in length	ten metres long or 10 m long
a disproportionate number	too few, or too many?[b]
for a further period of fifteen years	for another 15 years
if at all possible	if possible
an oral presentation	a talk *or* a presentation
I would have thought	I think
I myself would hope	I hope
during the month of April	in April
They are without any sanitary arrangements whatsoever.	They have no sanitation.
There really is somewhat of an obligation upon us to . . .	We ought to . . .
We are obliged to . . .	We must . . .
We are presently . . .	We are . . .
At the present time I am . . .	I am . . ..
a lot of information condensed into a very little amount of space	a lot of information in a small space
No admittance to unauthorised personnel	No admittance!

Notes
a   The abstract nouns in italics in column 1 are indicators of jargon (see page 72).
b   Be precise when you can. Say how many.

to *blame,* or where to begin to *reform.* We all value one another so much, upon this beautiful deceit; and labour for so long after it, in the years of our education: that we cannot but ever after think kinder of it, than it deserves.

Table 6.4 Some phrases that should not be used if one word would serve your purpose better[a]

Circumlocution English	Better English	Circumlocution	Better
make an adjustment	adjust	it would appear that	apparently
on an annual *basis*	yearly	owing to the *fact* that	because
in between	between	in all other *cases*	otherwise
check on	check	it may well be that	perhaps
count up	count	by the same token	similarly
arrive at a decision	decide	has an ability to	can
dusty in *character*	dusty	is not in a *position* to	cannot
make an examination	examine	in connection with	about
with the exception of	except	with regard to	about
for the purpose of	for	aimed at	for
if it is assumed that	if	entertainment value	fun
if and when	if (or when)	in the *event* that	if
at a later date	later[b]	in the *vicinity* of	near
later on	later[b]	a sufficient number	enough[b]
of a reversible *nature*	reversible	a small number of	few[b]
in order to	to	a smaller number of	fewer[b]
until such time as	until	limited in amount	small?
in conjunction with	with	a number of	several[b]
on a regular *basis*	regularly[b]	a high *degree* of	much[b]
remember that	remember	a great *deal* of	much[b]
located in	in	a *proportion* of	some[b]
situated on	on	a smaller amount of	less[b]
at the present *time*	now	prior to	before[b]
at that point in *time*	then	a greater length of time	longer[b]
in this day and age	now	the writing *process*	writing
on two occasions	twice	come to the conclusion	conclude
in most *cases*	usually	take into consideration	consider
during the time that	while	give positive encouragement to	encourage
somewhat costly	expensive	conduct an investigation into	investigate
under the name of	called	it is apparent therefore that	hence
of a reversible *nature*	reversible	on account of the fact that	because
spell out in depth	explain	bring to a conclusion	finish
seal off	seal	to say nothing of	and
with the *result* that	so	using a combination of	with

Notes
a The abstract nouns in italics are indicators of jargon (see page 72).
b Be precise when you can (say where, when, how much, how many, how often).

Reasons for verbosity

Tautology, circumlocution, ambiguity and verbosity arise from ignorance of the exact meaning of words, from lack of thought when writing, and from lack of care when revising. Also, people may use too few words when they speak, or too many words when they write, if they have not considered the difference between speaking and writing.

Graham Greene (1969) wrote in *Travels With My Aunt*: 'Human communication, it seems to me, involves an exaggerated amount of time. How briefly and to the point people always seem to speak on the stage or on the screen, while in real life we stumble from phrase to phrase with endless repetition'.

In conversation we may use more or fewer words than would be needed in writing. On the one hand, we use words to separate important ideas, we repeat things for emphasis, and we correct ourselves as we talk in an attempt to achieve greater precision. The extra words give listeners time to think. On the other hand, in conversation we take short cuts and leave out words when we see that the listener has understood and we have said enough. We can do this because as we talk we also communicate without words, by a body language in which every little movement has a meaning of its own.

In writing we must allow for the lack of direct contact with the reader, and use as many words as are needed to convey our thoughts precisely. Emphasis is usually made without repetition, and necessary pauses come from punctuation marks and paragraph breaks.

In writing, as in speaking, use words with which you are familiar and try to match your style to the occasion and to the needs of your readers. Write as you would speak to the audience you have in mind, but recognise that good spoken English is not the same as good written English. If a good talk is recorded and then published verbatim, readers may find that it is not good prose.

The use of more words than are needed, in writing, may result from a confusion of thought, a failure to take writing seriously, or laziness in sentence construction and revision. But most people, if they take the trouble, can write better than they normally talk – because in writing they have more time for thought and the opportunity to revise their work.

Apart from failure to consider the difference between speech and writing, and lack of care, there are other reasons why people fill their writing with empty words. Some seem to think that restatement in longer words is explanation. Others are trying to make a little knowledge go a long way. And others may even be trying to obscure meaning because they have nothing to say, or do not wish to commit themselves.

> 'Do, as a concession to my poor wits, Lord Darlington, just explain to me what you really mean.'

> 'I think I had better not, Duchess. Nowadays to be intelligible is to be found out.'

> *Lady Windermere's Fan*, Oscar Wilde (1892)

... only the wealthy, the capable, or the pretty can afford the luxury of saying right out just what they think, and blow the consequences.

Lieutenant Bones, Edgar Wallace (1918)

Wordiness may also result from affectation, from the studied avoidance of simplicity, in the belief that Latin phrases, long words and elaborate sentences appear learned (McCartney, 1953).

In a memorandum written early in the Second World War, Winston Churchill asked the heads of all government departments to cut out such phrases as 'It is also of importance to bear in mind the following considerations. . .' or 'Consideration should be given to the possibility of carrying into effect . . .' or to replace them by a single word. He emphasised that the discipline of setting out the real points concisely would prove an aid to clearer thinking.

Similarly, George Orwell (1946) complained about: (a) the use of foreign words and expressions simply for effect, (b) the use of such resounding commonplaces as *greatly to be desired, cannot be left out of account, a development to be expected in the near future, deserving of serious consideration* and *brought to a satisfactory conclusion*, to save the ends of sentences from anticlimax, and (c) the use of such high-sounding words as *basic, categorical, constitute, effective, element, exhibit, exploit, individual* (as a noun), *objective, phenomenon, primary, promote, utilise* and *virtual* to dress up simple statements and give an air of scientific impartiality to biased judgements.

Simplicity is the outward sign of clarity of thought. Wordiness, therefore, is a reflection on a writer's thinking, and a means by which writers conceal their meaning even from themselves. In an essay on style, Samuel Coleridge (1772–1834) wrote: 'If men would only say what they have to say in plain terms, how much more eloquent they would be'. Similarly, in *Our Language* (1966) Simeon Potter wrote: 'We shall be effective . . . as writers if we can say clearly, simply, and attractively just what we want to say and nothing more'.

Another cause of verbosity is that some people think that objectivity is achieved by writing in the passive voice; or they consider it impolite to refer to oneself directly. The repeated use of the personal pronouns I or we is undesirable, but avoiding them increases the number of words required (see Table 6.5) and can make the writing less rather than more objective. To write *We observed* or *I discovered*, for example, also has the advantage of making clear who was involved – and is to be preferred to such expressions as *It was found that*. Similarly, it is not always clear who is meant by *the author* or *the writers* (instead of *I* or *We*).

Table 6.5 Examples of the use of the active and passive voice

Prefer the active voice . . .	to the passive voice
We all have to read a mass of papers.	A mass of papers has to be read.
I ask my colleagues and their staffs to . . .	My colleagues and their staffs are asked to . . .
We received the following suggestions.	The following suggestions were received.
The proposal is . . .	What is being proposed is . . .

A reader's thoughts should move smoothly from each paragraph to the next, but many introductory phrases and connectives can be deleted without altering the meaning of a sentence or disrupting the smooth flow of language. Deleting such superfluous phrases (see Tables 4.1 and 5.1) will make your writing more direct and easier to read – and so more likely to serve your purpose. See also *Emphasis*, page 102.

Similarly, do not use more words than are needed in text references to tables and diagrams. For example, the introductory phrases 'It is clear from a consideration of Table . . . that . . .', and 'Figure . . . shows that. . .' are not necessary. They may also cause readers to think that in the table or figure they need note only one thing. It is better to say whatever you wish to say about the table or figure and then to refer to it by its number (in parenthesis), as in this book. It is also unnecessary in the heading to a table or the legend to a figure, to write: 'Table showing . . .' or 'Figure showing . . .' Any such superfluous words should be deleted when checking a composition.

However, in practising an economy of words, do not make the mistake of using too few words. As well as the words needed to convey your meaning, help readers follow your train of thought by including comment words (for example, *clearly*, *even*, *as expected* and *unexpected*) and connecting words (for example, *first*, *second*, *then*, *therefore*, *hence*, *however*, *moreover*, *nevertheless*, *on the contrary*, *as a result*, *similarly*, *so*, *thus*, *but*, *on the one hand* and *on the other hand*).

Where necessary, provide reminders to ensure the readers always know why what you are saying is relevant to your message. Your message should neither be obscured by a smokescreen of superfluous words nor deprived of words needed to give it strength. The rule must be to use the number of words needed to convey each thought precisely (without ambiguity). Brevity should not be achieved at the expense of accuracy, clarity, interest and coherence.

Improve your writing

Be clear and concise

1 Use standard English, or standard American English (see page 71).
2 Express your meaning in your own words (see pages 39–40).
3 Prefer one word to a phrase if the one word conveys your meaning clearly (see Table 6.4).
4 Include comment words and connecting words if they will help your readers to follow your train of thought (see page 78).
5 Use enough words to ensure efficient communication: neither more nor fewer than are needed to serve your purpose (see pages 72–3).

Cover Table 6.1 with a sheet of paper, then uncover column 1 and for each entry consider where the word *only* should be placed to convey the meaning the author presumably intended.

Cover Table 6.3 with a sheet of paper, then uncover column 1 and for each entry suggest how the meaning could be better expressed in fewer words.

Cover Table 6.4 with a sheet of paper, then uncover column headed 'Circumlocution' and suggest one word that should be preferred to the phrase in each entry. Continue to the end of this table.

Read to understand

Exercises in comprehension

Comprehension means understanding. Your understanding of any writing depends partly on the author's clarity of expression and partly on your vocabulary. Exercises in comprehension can be set in teaching any subject, and in tests and examinations, to find out whether or not students understand words and phrases used in a particular context. You should answer comprehension questions concisely – in your own words.

Exercises in comprehension stimulate thought and provide opportunities for discussion in which you learn not only about writing but also about your subject. They should therefore be set by teachers of other subjects as well as by teachers of English.

Bear in mind that every question set in coursework and examinations is a comprehension test. Unless you understand the exact meaning of each word used in any question (see also page 67), you cannot be confident that you understand the question and are preparing a complete and correct answer.

Read to summarise

When you read, as a student or in other employment, you must recognise the points that are important for your work. These may, for example, be added to your lecture notes or listed on an index card as revision aids (see page 131). The ability to write précis and summaries will be useful when you take notes, and as you collect ideas from different sources when planning one of your own compositions. With experience in writing précis and summaries you may also take more care with your own choice and use of words as you develop a more direct and forceful style of writing.

How to prepare a précis

Read the original twice before starting your précis: first to ensure that you understand every sentence, and again as you select and note the main points – reconstructing the author's topic outline. Consider the author's purpose and then choose an effective heading for your précis. Keep this heading in mind as you prepare a rough draft based on your notes. Then check your précis against the original, making sure that it is in good English, not in note form, and that the writer of the original is acknowledged and accurately reported. With practice you will grasp the essentials of a composition at first reading and so will find précis writing easier.

Preparing a précis is a test of comprehension and an exercise in reduction, in which the essential meaning of a composition is retained – omitting anything of secondary importance, all figurative language, all digressions and all superfluous words. The order of presentation should not be changed unless it is faulty: the author's meaning should be conveyed in your own words – and in fewer words.

As part of a course in scholarly writing, students could be asked (a) to prepare a précis of an article relevant to their studies, working alone, and then (b) to try to agree as to which words in the article can be omitted in the précis.

How to prepare a summary

A summary should be much shorter than a précis (see page 165). It should include only the author's main points: it is like a topic outline – but written in complete sentences. So, preparing a summary is a good test of your ability to recognise these main points, and to incorporate them in your lecture notes or report them in a few well-chosen words in one of your own compositions (see *Citing sources of information*, page 132).

For practice in preparing a summary, select an article relevant to your own work from a recent issue of a magazine or journal in which authors' summaries are published. Before looking at the author's summary, read the article carefully, listing the main points, and then prepare your own summary (in less than 200 words). Do you agree with the author's choice of the most important points? Has the author used more words than are needed? Have you?

Because it is easier to criticise and condense other people's writing than your own (see *Read critically*, page 26), preparing précis and summaries provides practice in recognising important points and will help you (a) to look critically at the first draft of each composition you prepare to see if you can improve it by making it more concise, and so (b) to develop a clear, simple and direct style that is appropriate for most scholarly writing.

How to write a book review

Many journals and magazines contain reviews of books likely to be of interest to their readers, written by suitably qualified reviewers. A book review is also a useful exercise in comprehension and criticism for students interested in the art of writing. Before writing a book review, read the book. Make brief notes, remembering that to criticise does not mean to find fault with. Criticism of a good book or a good play should be favourable.

The length of a book review may be decided by the editor; and if the review is too long it may be reduced by the editor. The easiest way to do this is to remove sentences at the end – so the most important things must come first and the least important last. The reader needs: title of book (and sub-title); name(s) of author(s) or editor(s) from the title page; date of publication from the title page verso; number of edition (unless the first); name of publisher; place of publication; total number of pages (including preliminary pages); number of tables and figures; and price of hardback and of paperback.

Readers of a book review have been attracted by the title. They do not want a précis or summary of the book. They do want a brief guide and evaluation, to help them to decide whether or not to look at the book. Answer the following questions. What is the book about, if this is not obvious from the title? Has it any special features? How is the subject treated? What prior knowledge is assumed? For whom is the author writing? Is the treatment comprehensive? Is the book interesting and easy to read? Are the illustrations effective? Is the book well organised? Will the reader, for whom the book is intended, find the book useful? How does the book compare with similar books (if there are any) or with the author's earlier works?

Reviewers who have never written a book are unlikely to appreciate the writer's difficulties. Perhaps this is why some reviewers seem to be looking for the perfect book. Although a reviewer may choose to draw attention to errors, if these indicate that the author is not as knowledgeable as he or she should be, it is not the reviewer's task to list every minor fault. Nor is it the purpose of a book review to show that the reviewer is (or is not) clever and witty, and could have written a better book. However, a review that is intended for publication should begin or end with the name of the reviewer – who will probably be well known to readers of the newspaper or journal in which the review is published.

Edit the work of others

You will probably find it easier to recognise long words that could be replaced by short words, phrases that could be deleted, and sentences that are verbose, when you read someone else's writing than when you try to revise your own. However, as a result of editing the writing of others you will start to take more care in revising your own. Each of the following extracts is followed by comments, and by suggestions as to how it could be improved. Cover the comments and suggestions while you consider each extract. Then write your own edited version before you consider mine.

Extract from a letter from an editor

This is to inform you that we have received your manuscript entitled . . .
Although we found it interesting . . .   17 words

COMMENTS

1   The words 'This is to inform you' can be omitted without altering the meaning of the sentence.
2   Obviously the manuscript has been received, otherwise there could be no reply.

EDITED VERSION

Thank you for sending your manuscript entitled . . .
We found it interesting, but . . .   12 words

Extract from a book on writing

Indeed it could be said that personal advancement in life lies in the ability to say the right kind of words in the right way at the right time.   29 words

COMMENTS

1   The words 'it could be said that' add nothing to the meaning of this sentence.
2   Personal advancement must be in life, so the words 'in life' are not needed.
3   Most people would say 'the right things', not 'the right kind of words'.

EDITED VERSION

Indeed, personal advancement depends on the ability to say the right things, in the right way, at the right time.   20 words

Extract from another book on writing

People often read instructions only as a last resort, when they can no longer manage without them.   17 words

COMMENTS

1   The first four words convey the opposite of the intended message.
2   The words 'People often' are used when the words 'Many people' are required.
3   The problem is not that people often read instructions but that many people do not read them at all.

EDITED VERSION

Many people do not read instructions – except as a last resort when they can no longer manage without them.   20 words

Extract from the newsletter of a professional institute

During the development of the Continuing Personal Development scheme we presented it to various employers and engaged in consultation and discussion to facilitate a good degree of integration between our scheme and existing employer schemes.   35 words

COMMENTS

1   Why not say how many employers were consulted?
2   A presentation includes discussion, as does a consultation.

3   The phrase a good degree of is uninformative, as would be any imprecise word such as considerable, much or some (see *Use numbers
when you can be precise*, page 85).
4   The word degree is an indicator of jargon (see words printed in italics
in Tables 6.3 and 6.4).
5   Many more words are used than are needed in this article about the
development of key skills, including the ability to communicate.

EDITED VERSION

We discussed the plans for our Personal Development Scheme with several
employers to ensure that, as far as possible, it will satisfy their requirements.

24 words

But, instead of several, say how many!

7 Using numbers, tables and illustrations

In some subjects, including those concerned with the study of language and literature, it is usual to convey one's thoughts using words alone. In other subjects, tables and illustrations make it possible to convey information and ideas that could not be presented adequately in words alone: clearly, precisely and quickly – either without words or using fewer words than would otherwise be needed.

Use numbers when you can be precise

A politician may say that a fund will be established, 'of *substantial* size, and *adequate* coverage over a *considerable* period'. Such vague words are used to express hopes when it is impossible to be either certain or precise.

Consider the meaning you wish to convey before using the word *very* with an adverb (very quickly) or with an adjective (very large), and before using adverbs (for example, *slowly*) or adjectives (for example, *small, appreciable, large* and *heavy*) or modifying and intensifying words (for example, *comparatively, exceptionally, extremely, fairly, quite, rather, really, relatively* and *unduly*). Vague statements do not help readers, and are likely to annoy them.

> Whenever anyone says I can do something soon I'll say to them yes, I know all about that . . ., but when, when, when?
>
> *Key to the Door*, Alan Sillitoe (1961)

Using numbers in written work

In your writing, be precise whenever you can. Instead of vague words, use numbers to make clear how many; and use numbers followed by appropriate units of measurement to indicate exact quantities: how far, how long, how heavy, how thick.

Use arabic numerals (not words) for the day and for the year, when writing dates, but name the month so that you cannot be misunderstood. For example, write 04 June 2020 or 4th June 2020, not 04.06.2020 (day, month, year) or, for the same day, 06.04.2020 (month, day, year).

Roman numerals are no longer used for numbering photographs or tables; so their only use in scholarly writing is to identify monarchs (for example, Queen Elizabeth II as an alternative to Queen Elizabeth the Second) and popes.

Because of differences in their meaning in different countries, do not use the words billion, trillion and quadrillion.

Hyphenate cardinal numbers (twenty-one to ninety-nine) and ordinal numbers (for example, twenty-first, one-hundred-and-first), and fractions (for example, two-thirds, one-sixth).

Except in scientific and technical writing, or when they are included in tables, write numbers less than 100 in words, and prefer words to symbols. However, (a) prefer figures to words if different items are listed in the same sentence, and (b) to avoid ambiguity, never write two numbers together, either as figures or words (for example, write two 50 W lamps, not 2 50 W lamps and not two fifty watt lamps).

Always use words if a number is necessary at the beginning of a sentence. And, even in scientific writing, use words for numbers one to nine – except before a symbol (six metres or 6 m) or before a percentage sign (six per cent in the text, but 6% in a table or diagram).

Where necessary, define percentages (for example, when describing solutions distinguish percentage by mass from percentage by volume).

In some countries a decimal point is indicated by a full stop on the line (not by a point raised above the line). In other countries a decimal point is indicated by a comma; so do not use commas to break large numbers into groups of three digits. Write numbers up to 9999 without a comma, and leave spaces instead of commas to break numbers with more than four digits into groups of three digits above or below the decimal point (for example: write 999 999 and 10 000 but 9999). However, in a list of numbers, decimal points and spaces must be in vertical alignment (which explains why there is a space between the 8 and the 5 in the number 8 564 in Table 7.2 but no space in the other four-digit numbers in this table).

Using International System units

Most countries use the International System of Units (Système International d'Unités, abbreviated to SI units). In this system, the magnitude of any physical quantity is stated as the product of a pure number and an SI unit (physical quantity = number × unit).

Table 7.1 Some International System units of measurement (SI units)*

Quantity	Unit of measurement	Symbol
length	millimetre (0.001 m)	mm
	centimetre (0.01 m)	cm
	metre	m
	kilometre (1000 m)	km
area	square centimetre	cm^2
	square metre	m^2
	hectare (10 000 m^2)	ha
	square kilometre (100 ha)	km^2
volume	cubic centimetre	cm^3
	cubic metre	m^3
capacity	millilitre (0.001 l)	ml
	litre	l
mass	gram (0.001 kg)	g
	kilogram	kg
	metric tonne (1000 kg)	t
density	kilogram per cubic metre	kg/m^3
time	second	s
	minute (60 s)	min
	hour	h
	day	d
speed/velocity	metres per second	m/s
	kilometres per second	km/s
temperature	degree Celsius	°C

Note
* The International System of Units includes base units (e.g. the metre, kilogram, and second) and derived units (e.g. the centimetre and gram). The litre, tonne, minute, hour, day and degree Celsius are recognised units outside the International System. The hectare is accepted temporarily in view of existing practice. In Britain the degree Celsius used to be called the degree centigrade. For more information on SI units, including units not shown in this table, see the British Standard BS 5555 or the identical International Standard ISO 1000.

When using the symbols for SI units of measurement, instead of words (see Table 7.1 and the footnote), the following rules apply:

1   Leave a space between the number and the symbol (for example, 50 W and 20 °C).
2   Do not put a full stop after the symbol unless it comes at the end of a sentence.
3   Do not add an s to any symbol. With SI units the same symbol is used for both singular and plural (for example, m = metre or metres; ms = millisecond or milliseconds).

Use tables and illustrations to help you explain

Tables and illustrations help to break up pages of writing, provide variety and stimulate interest. They capture attention and so should be used to emphasise important points: enabling you to communicate information or ideas clearly, concisely, precisely, forcefully and quickly – with fewer words than would otherwise be needed.

Consider tables and illustrations as part of your composition, therefore, not as ornament. Ensure that they complement your writing. Do not add them at the end as if they were an afterthought or mere decoration. Instead, when planning a composition, consider how best information or ideas can be conveyed – to the readers you have in mind – in words, tables or illustrations.

Information presented in one way (for example, in a table) should not also be presented in another way in the same composition (as it is in this chapter to facilitate comparison of different methods of presentation (compare Table 7.2 with Figure 7.8, and Figure 7.2 with Figure 7.7). Instead, depending on your purpose and the needs of your readers, include information once only: in the text, in a table or in an illustration. By planning, avoid repetition and ensure that each table and each illustration is:

1   numbered;
2   arranged so that, if possible, it fits upright (portrait, not landscape) on the page and can be viewed without the reader having to rotate the page;
3   placed near the relevant text;
4   referred to at least once in the text, with any necessary explanation and with cross-references included in other (usually later) parts of the composition if these will help readers; and
5   prepared before you start to write so that you can look at it as you write, refer to it in your composition, and write fewer words than you would otherwise need.

Tables

In a table words and numbers are arranged for easy reference, usually in columns. For example, a table of contents is a list of headings and page numbers – to help readers see how a composition is organised and to help them find parts that may be of interest. Other tables are useful, especially in extended essays and project reports (see page 160), because they allow you to provide additional relevant information, concisely, without interrupting the flow of words.

Table 7.2 The world: people and land use

World region	Population[a] (millions)		Surface area [b] (000s km^2)
	1950	*2000*	
Africa	224	796	30 250
North America	166	316	21 776
Latin America	166	520	20 546
Asia	1403	3680	31 879
Europe	549	728	22 050
Oceania	13	31	8 564
World totals	2520	6071	135 065

Notes
a Estimates for each world region from *UN Demographic Yearbook 2001*, New York, United Nations.
b Land surface includes unproductive areas.

The tables in any document should be placed appropriately and numbered consecutively. Each table should be on a separate sheet, with a clear and concise heading (above the table, as in Table 7.2) and with sub-headings if these will help the reader (as in Table 1.1).

Readers should be able to understand the tables without reading the text, but at least one cross-reference to each table should be included in the text (as in the previous sentence). The information provided in a table should not be repeated in the text, or in an illustration, and a table should not include columns of numbers that could be calculated easily from numbers in other columns.

The size of each table should be decided in relation to the size and shape of the page or column in which it is to fit. If possible, it should fit upright on the page so that readers can look from the text to the table without having to rotate the page.

The first column on the left of a table is called the stub. This labels the horizontal rows of the table, indicating what the investigator has decided to study (called the independent variable). In a table used to record numerical data or the results of the analysis of such data, the stub could, for example, state the times at which readings were taken, the names of individuals or nations, or (as in Table 7.2) the world regions selected for study.

The data or results recorded in other columns of a table, the values of which will depend on changes in the independent variable, indicate changes in the dependent variables. There is one column for each dependent variable studied, as indicated by concise column headings – which must include units of measurement for every quantity shown (see Table 7.2). If there is no entry in any part of a table, this should be shown by three dots . . . and a footnote stating that no information is available. A nought should be used only for a zero reading.

In a table, comparison should be possible both vertically and horizontally; and where a total is given in the bottom right-hand corner, the vertical and horizontal totals must agree. In most tables information can be presented clearly without horizontal or vertical ruled lines.

Any necessary footnotes should be immediately below the table to which they apply, but – whether the document is handwritten or word processed – there should normally be no other material on the same page. Each footnote should be preceded by a superscript reference symbol or letter (as in Tables 7.1 and 7.2), not by a number. These reference symbols or letters must also be included in the table, in superscript, to identify the entries to which the footnotes refer (as in Tables 7.1 and 7.2).

If tables of original data are necessary, for example in a report, these are best placed in an appendix so that they are readily available for reference without distracting the readers' attention from your argument in the text. In contrast, most text tables should be concise summaries (results of the analysis of data, see page 55), to provide readers with just the information they need and to help you to make a point.

Whether tables are in the text or in an appendix, horizontal and vertical ruled lines should be included only if they will help readers. In most text tables vertical ruled lines are not necessary; and instead of horizontal ruled lines the parts of a table can be indicated by concise sub-headings or separated by leaving extra space between horizontal rows.

Illustrations

Different kinds of illustrations, which may be photographs, drawings or diagrams, are all called figures. They should be numbered consecutively in any composition, separately from the tables.

Each illustration should have a concise caption or legend – immediately below the figure – so that readers can understand the illustration without reference to the text, and so that the source of any data or artwork that is not original can be acknowledged.

In a handwritten composition, especially in an examination, simple illustrations are best prepared quickly as you write, using coloured pencils to draw attention to different points of interest.

If pen and ink drawings are necessary, for example in a project report or thesis, draw them twice their final dimensions – with lines twice as thick – for photographic reduction by half.

If a drawing for any document is also to be used in preparing slides for projection, its width will depend on the page width of the document but the proportions of the drawing for a 5 × 5 cm slide must be 3:4 (portrait) or 4:3 (landscape).

Your artwork will usually be in black on a white background. The use of colour for artwork, especially on a coloured background, can cause problems for some readers (for example, as a result of colour blindness) and artwork on a coloured background may be lost if an illustration has to be reproduced in monochrome.

To help readers, if two or more illustrations are to be compared they must be to the same scale, whether they are prepared with pen and ink or using computer graphic software (see page 188), and if possible they should be arranged side by side.

If symbols or different kinds of shading are used in any diagram they must either be explained in the legend (as in Figure 7.7) or, preferably, in a key provided as part of the diagram (as in Figures 7.2 and 7.8) so that the symbols are not lost if the illustration is later reproduced without the legend in another document

Photographs

A photograph enables readers to see things that otherwise would have to be described, so it reduces the number of words required. It serves the double function of depiction and corroboration. However, readers may be too easily convinced that what they see in a photograph is necessarily correct. A photograph cannot lie but it may mislead. This is especially likely when natural shadows, which give a three-dimensional effect, are destroyed by artificial lighting. Furthermore, even an excellent photograph may lose some details in reproduction. So if you decide to use photographs, for example in a project report, look at each one for relevance, interest, sharpness of focus, and effective lighting and contrast. Then consider whether or not a good drawing or diagram would serve your purpose better.

Drawings

Line drawings are used in reports of practical work, with each line intended as an accurate record of an observation. If the proportions are to be correct such a drawing must be to scale, and a scale must be marked on the drawing in metric units. Preparing a line drawing is therefore an aid to observation (see page 15), and each line is a summary of observations (see Figure 7.1).

Instead of shading, in a line drawing use effective labelling to direct attention to different structures or parts. The labelling lines should be

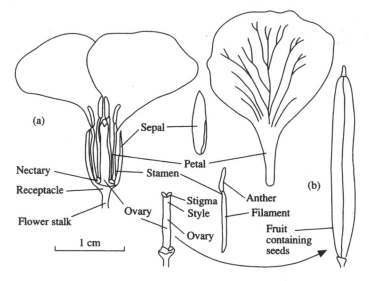

Figure 7.1 A line drawing: preparing a drawing is an aid to observation, and an annotated drawing is an aid to concise description: (a) the parts of a flower of *Cheiranthus cheiri*, the wallflower, and (b) the fruit that develops from the ovary. Diagram from Barrass, R. (1982) *Modern Biology*, London, Heinemann.

drawn by placing a pencil point on the thing to be labelled and, using a rule, drawing a straight line away from this point. Labelling lines should not cross one another, and should radiate from the drawing so that they are well spaced and the illustration as a whole (drawing and labelling) is well balanced. Arrowheads should not be used on labelling lines, because (a) it may not be obvious to readers whether the arrowheads end on or point to the structures to be labelled, and (b) in many drawings and diagrams arrows are used for other purposes.

In a drawing, as in a photograph, three-dimensional objects are represented in two dimensions. The drawing represents things as they are seen at one time from one place. A drawing, therefore, although it is intended to help readers, could be misleading. For many purposes a diagram is better.

Graphs and charts

Diagrams used for presenting numerical data, or results of the analysis of such data, include line graphs, histograms, bar charts and pie charts.

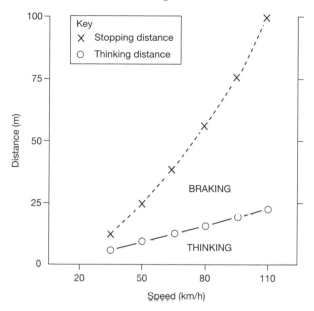

Figure 7.2 Graph or line chart: thinking and stopping distances for cars travelling at different speeds. These are the shortest stopping distances for alert drivers of cars with good brakes and tyres, on dry roads. Based on data from *The Highway Code*, London, HMSO. Compare with Figure 7.7.

Line graphs (also called line charts). A line graph shows how one thing varies relative to changes in another. The variable decided by the investigator (for example, in Figure 7.2, the vehicle speeds at which stopping distances are to be recorded) is called the independent variable and must be plotted in relation to the horizontal axis (the *x* axis). The other variable, which the investigator cannot decide in advance (for example, the stopping distance), and which depends on changes in the independent variable, is called the dependent variable and is plotted in relation to the vertical axis (the y axis).

A statement in the legend should indicate whether the points on the graph marked by symbols (usually by ○ or × or +) represent records of observations (data, as in a scatter diagram) or average values (as in Figure 7.2). If the latter, either the standard error ($\pm S\bar{x}$) or the 5 per cent fiducial limits of error in the mean ($\pm 1.96\ S\bar{x}$) may be shown by a vertical line through the mean, with a note in the legend to indicate which is represented.

The scales on the axes of a graph should normally start from zero: they should be chosen carefully and marked clearly. If it is impracticable to start

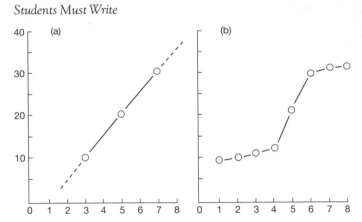

Figure 7.3 How interpolation (based on insufficient evidence) and extrapolation
(based on the imagination) can be misleading. (a) Unbroken lines
show interpolation; broken lines, extrapolation. (b) How additional
readings could affect your interpretation.

the scale from zero, the break in the axis should be clearly indicated by a
jagged line. All numbers should be upright but the labelling of the scales
should be parallel to the axes (as in Figure 7.2). Units of measurement must
be stated. The diagram as a whole is the graph (line chart) and the lines on
the graph, representing trends, even if they are best-fitting straight lines,
are called curves.

Joining the points on a graph by lines (as do the unbroken lines in Figure
7.3a) is called interpolation; and continuing a line beyond the points on a
graph (as do the broken lines in Figure 7.3a) is called extrapolation. Figure
7.3b illustrates how extra readings (additional evidence) could affect your
interpretation of the results represented in Figure 7.3a. Both interpolation
and extrapolation are speculation, which may mislead the writer as well as
the reader. A remark by Winston Churchill, made in another context, is
appropriate: 'It is wise to look ahead but foolish to look further than you
can see'.

Histograms. A histogram can be used to represent a frequency distribution in which the variation in the data is continuous (meaning that the
observations recorded do not fall into distinct or discrete groups). As in a
graph, the independent variable being studied (for example, the age at
which people started smoking in Figure 7.4) is plotted in relation to the
horizontal axis: the number on the left of each vertical column indicates
the lowest measurement included in that grouping interval. The vertical

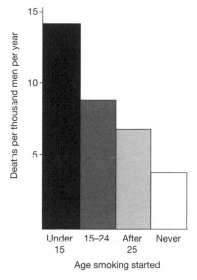

Figure 7.4 Histogram: dying for a smoke. Number of deaths each year per 1000 men (aged 45 to 54) in the United States. The earlier a man starts to smoke the more likely he is to die before the age of 54. Based on results of Hammond, E. C., in *National Cancer Institute Monograph* (1966).

column for each grouping interval shows the frequency of observations in that interval. Adjacent columns touch, indicating that the variation is continuous. Note that the scale on the vertical axis starts from zero. As with a graph, all numbers should be upright but the labelling of the scales should be parallel to the axes (as in Figure 7.4).

Bar charts. A *vertical bar chart*, also called a *column graph* or *column chart*, can be used to represent a frequency distribution in which the variation in the data is discontinuous (the observations recorded do fall into discrete groups). As with line graphs and histograms, the variable being studied (the independent variable) is plotted in relation to the horizontal axis, and the length of a vertical column or bar indicates the frequency of observations in each group (the number of a dependent variable at different times, in different groups or places, or under different conditions).

Adjacent columns should be labelled separately and should not touch, emphasising that the variation is discontinuous. As the data are discrete, there is no difficulty in assigning each observation to a group. For example, the number of children in a family or the number of rhinoceros in a locality must be a whole number.

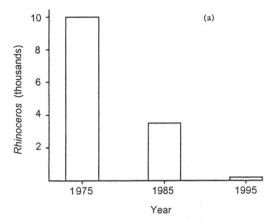

Figure 7.5 (a) Column graph or vertical bar chart: *Rhinoceros* in Zimbabwe.
Estimates from Bridgland, 'The end of the rhino', *Sunday Telegraph
Review*, 11 December 1994.

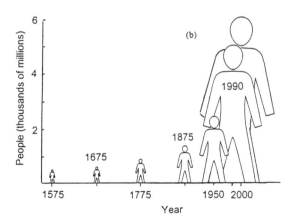

Figure 7.5 (b) Pictogram: world population growth 1575–2000. Note that
population size is represented by the height of each symbol, not by
its area (see text). Estimates from *UN Demographic Yearbook 2001*,
New York, United Nations.

The columns must be rectangles (as in Figure 7.5a) because it is the
height of a column, not its area, that corresponds to the quantity represented. Drawings should not be used instead of columns (as in Figure
7.5b) because differences in the area of the drawings are likely to mislead
readers.

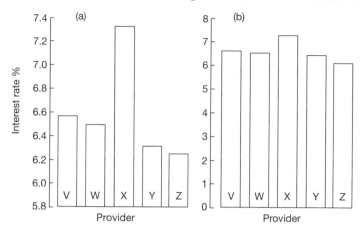

Figure 7.6 How a graph or chart with a false or suppressed zero can be misleading. Vertical bar charts: (a) chart with suppressed zero, which could cause some readers to think that the rate of interest from provider X was more than twice that available from some of its competitors; (b) chart with a scale that does not exaggerate differences between the interest rates available from these five providers.

Readers may also be misled if a scale on a graph, histogram or other kind of chart does not start from zero. The zero is said to be suppressed or false, and this can make a small difference appear greater than it actually is. Some readers may consider an illustration with a suppressed zero, or with an otherwise inappropriate scale, to be a deliberate attempt to mislead them (compare Figure 7.6a, based on an advertisement, with Figure 7.6b).

In non-technical writing a column chart may be drawn on its side (as a *horizontal bar chart*, with the dependent variable represented on the horizontal axis) if horizontal bars are more appropriate, make more impact, and so help to convey a message more effectively (see Figure 7.7).

In a *pictorial bar chart* (see Figure 7.8) the bars are replaced by identical symbols (with a key as part of the diagram to indicate what each symbol represents). Note that, as in this illustration, a bar chart can be used to show how one or more things vary in relation to another when one of the variables is geographical or qualitative (not numerical): for example, (a) in different world regions (as in Figure 7.8) and (b) in a chart used in planning one's work (as in Figure 11.2).

Pie charts. In a pie chart (also known as a *sector chart, circle chart* or *circular graph*) slices of the pie (sectors) are arranged in order according to their size, clockwise, starting at noon with the largest slice (and each slice

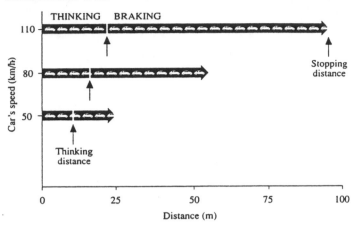

Figure 7.7 Horizontal bar chart: thinking and stopping distances for cars travelling at different speeds. These are the shortest stopping distances for alert drivers of cars with good brakes and tyres, on dry roads. Speed, decided by the driver, should be plotted in relation to the horizontal axis of a graph (as in Figure 7.2), but this chart is drawn on its side for visual effect – and greater impact. Distances are shown in metres and also in car lengths. Based on data from *The Highway Code*, London, HMSO.

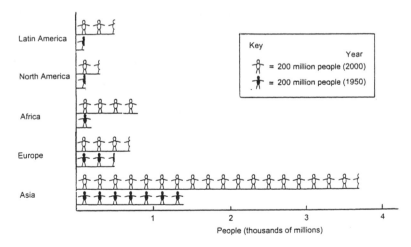

Figure 7.8 Pictorial bar chart: population growth in different world regions between 1950 and 2000 (estimates also presented in Table 7.2). Note that Oceania (Australia, New Zealand, and the Pacific Islands excluding Hawaii) cannot be represented because (see Table 7.2) only one-eighth of a symbol would be required. Estimates for each world region from UN *Demographic Yearbook 2001*, New York, United Nations.

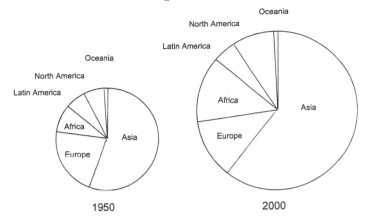

Figure 7.9 Circular graph or pie chart: where people lived in 1950 and in 2000. The difference in size (area) of these two charts represents the fact that the world population more than doubled in these 50 years. Estimates for each world region from UN *Demographic Yearbook 2001*, New York, United Nations.

representing a fraction of 360 degrees). For example, if 796 million people were living in Africa in the year 2000 and the world population was 6071 million, a 47° sector of the chart can be used to represent the population of Africa in 2000 (calculated by dividing 796 by 6071 and multiplying the result by 360).

If two pie charts are to be compared, the slices in the second should be arranged in the same order as in the first (as in Figure 7.9). The difference in the area of these two charts represents the difference in world population.

A pie chart can be effective in conveying a quick general impression (as does Figure 7.9). However, because small differences in the size of sectors are difficult to differentiate visually, they should not be represented in a pie chart; and no sector should be less than 7°. If the reader has to make accurate comparisons a chart that uses lines to represent information should be preferred, because it is easier to compare line lengths than areas. But if the reader needs exact numbers only a table will suffice.

Other kinds of diagram

Floor plans and *maps* drawn to scale and with a scale bar, convey more information – more accurately – than could photographs or line drawings.

A map is a kind of diagram, but there are difficulties in representing the curved surface of a globe to scale on a flat surface and readers who do not

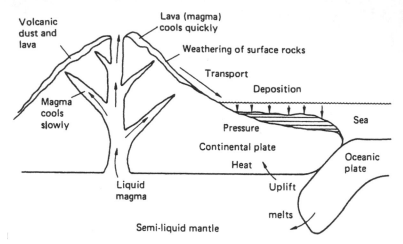

Figure 7.10 A line drawing as a summary of observations (made using the five
senses, aided by the use of scientific instruments): to help readers
visualise Earth's crust on a semi-liquid mantle, rock formation and
rock destruction. The diagram illustrates a key principle in geology,
the principle of uniformity: *What is happening now on Earth has
happened similarly in the past.* Diagram from Barrass, R. (1991) *Science*,
Basingstoke, Macmillan.

understand the projection used may be misled. On every map there should
be an arrow indicating north.

Some diagrams are not drawn to scale. In these each line is not intended
as an accurate record: it is the diagram as a whole that, for example, provides a useful summary of observations (as does Figure 7.10) or of ideas (as
does Figure 9.1), shows the arrangement of components in a piece of equipment (as does an electrical *circuit diagram*), represents successive stages in a
process (as does a *flow chart*), or helps people make decisions (as does an
algorithm or *decision chart*).

Algorithms. Algorithms help users, for example: (a) to make choices as
they carry out an activity (for example, when using a key for identifying
objects), to follow sequences (for example, when following a fault-finding
procedure, or at successive stages in a manufacturing process), or (b) to
understand connections or relationships (for example, in a hierarchical
organisation or in a family tree). Each algorithm is a set of instructions in
which the user is given a choice and has to make a decision at each step.

8   Helping your readers

By making things easy for your readers, you help yourself to convey information and ideas. You should therefore consider what you know about your readers and try to match your vocabulary and style of writing to their needs. This is easiest if you are a student writing for one reader or an employee writing to a colleague or to a customer whom you know well.

Even if you have not met your readers, anticipate their difficulties so that you can try to ensure that your writing will be understood at first reading by all those for whom it is intended.

Provide an informative title and, if appropriate, use headings and subheadings as signposts. Present information in an effective order; include all essential steps in any argument; give sufficient evidence in support of anything new; give examples, and explain why any point is particularly important.

No statement should be self-evident, but be as explicit as necessary. As a student, especially, you have to make clear your understanding. Do not leave your readers to work out the implications of any statement. Help them to appreciate the connection between sentences and paragraphs: in some places a word or phrase may be enough (see page 78); in others some explanation may be required.

Try not to mislead your readers. Make clear any assumptions underlying your arguments, because if these were incorrect your conclusions might also be incorrect. Take care that any assumptions, conjectures or possibilities are not later mentioned as if they were facts. Words to watch, because they may introduce an opinion, are *obviously*, *surely* and *of course*.

Fulfil your readers' expectations. For example: (a) follow the words *not only* by *but also*, *whether* by *or*, *on the one hand* by *on the other hand*, and *first* by *second*; and (b) if you list items, mention all or none of them in the sentences that follow. Otherwise, if only some are mentioned, your readers may be wondering about the others when they should be following your train of thought.

Write for easy reading

Your writing should be appropriate to the subject, to the needs of your readers, and to the occasion. Try to convey your thoughts clearly, accurately and impartially so that your readers take your meaning at first reading and always feel at ease.

How to begin

If you know what you would like to communicate but have difficulty in getting started, look at the opening sentences of similar compositions by other people. You could begin, for example, with a question or with an answer to one of your readers' questions (see page 33). But it is better to get started than to spend too much time trying to think of the most effective beginning: your best starting point will usually become apparent as you prepare your topic outline (see pages 34–6).

The only rules are: (a) leave no doubt about the purpose and scope of the composition – if this is not clear from the title – and in coursework and examinations make clear that you have begun your answer to the question set; (b) make your first paragraph short and to the point; and (c) start with things that you expect your readers to know and build on this foundation.

Control

Try to maintain the momentum of your writing. Do not dwell for too long on any topic, therefore, and make the connection between paragraphs clear. Apply the test of relevance to everything. Make sure that every word or phrase is appropriate to its context and that every sentence conveys a whole thought.

Good headings (see page 34) and paragraph breaks make for easy reading – but only if the headings and paragraphs are in an effective sequence that is obvious to the reader. Keeping control, therefore, depends first on your knowledge of the subject and then on careful planning (see page 41) so that you can deal fully with each topic in one place – presenting your thoughts in an appropriate, ordered and interesting way.

Emphasis

In speech, emphasis is achieved mainly by inflexions of the voice. In writing, mark in your topic outline the points you intend to emphasise – so that you can ensure they are sufficiently emphasised in your finished composition.

Emphasis is important in all writing and is present whether or not the writer is in control. But, to use emphasis effectively, a writer must know how to make the most important points stand out from the supporting detail. There are many ways in which, without the sound of your voice, you can draw attention to parts of a composition, particular sentences in a paragraph, and selected words in a sentence.

In coursework your title will usually be the question set; but in examinations you would write only the number of the question you are answering (because to copy out the question would be a waste of time). Always consider carefully the wording of the question or of your title, and of all your headings and sub-headings, to ensure that they serve to emphasise the purpose of the whole and of each part.

Devote one paragraph to each topic. Paragraphs are units of thought and will therefore vary in length (see page 37); but if the topics are of comparable importance you might expect to write paragraphs of similar length.

Plan effective diagrams if these will help you to convey the essential points of your composition (see page 88), or if they are necessary to enable you to convey information that cannot be conveyed by words alone.

Beginnings and endings are important. The first and last paragraphs (the introduction and conclusion – see pages 34 and 35) are those to which readers pay the most attention. The most important words in each paragraph are the first words and the last words, so miss out unnecessary introductory phrases (see Tables 4.1 and 4.2) and end each paragraph effectively.

The most important words in a sentence, for emphasis, come at the beginning and at the end. The first words direct the reader's attention. Because these first words are emphasised, a writer may use the same words to convey the same information and yet direct the readers' attention to different things. For example:

The first men on the moon were two United States astronauts, Neil Armstrong and Edward Aldrin.

Two United States astronauts, Neil Armstrong and Edward Aldrin, were the first men on the moon.

Neil Armstrong and Edward Aldrin, two United States astronauts, were the first men on the moon.

Asides, within a sentence, may be marked – according to the importance you place on them – by commas, dashes or curved brackets (as illustrated in this sentence). See also *Brackets and dashes*, page 199.

Underline words in your topic outline or in your own notes, to draw attention to important points. Otherwise, underline only (a) the subject headings of letters and memoranda, and (b) words that in a printed or word-processed document would be printed in italics (see page 184).

In books, it is usual to print in italics only: (a) the conjunctions *but*, *and*, *either . . . or . . .*, and *neither . . . nor . . .*, when used – as in examination questions – to emphasise an important distinction or contrast; (b) the titles of books, films, poems and plays (for example, write *Hamlet* the play, but Hamlet the man); (c) the names of newspapers, magazines and journals (for example, *The Times* newspaper); (d) the scientific names of genera (for example, the genus *Homo*) and species (for example, the species *Homo sapiens*); (e) the names of ships; and (f) words from a foreign language which although used in English are not accepted as English words (for example, *modus operandi* and *in loco parentis*).

Leave out anything that is irrelevant, not only because irrelevant material wastes your time and your reader's time but also because you must take care not to draw the reader's attention away from relevant material.

Use more forceful language for important points than for the supporting detail; and repeat important words.

Items of comparable importance, listed in a sentence, can be emphasised: by repeating a word (as in this sentence), by lower case letters in curved brackets (as on this page), by numbering (as on page 105), or by indentation (as on page 88). However, if a sentence or paragraph is well balanced, so that it reads well, emphasis will fall naturally on each part.

Long involved sentences may indicate that you have not thought sufficiently about what you are trying to say. However, this does not mean that all your sentences must be short. A long sentence, if properly constructed, may be easier to read than a succession of short ones. There is no rule that a sentence, when read aloud, should be read in one breath.

When learning a language, short sentences are the easiest to write and the easiest to read, but good prose is seldom written entirely in short sentences. Sentences vary in length. Short sentences are effective for introducing a new topic (as in three of the preceding paragraphs about emphasis), long sentences for developing a point, and short sentences for emphasising each step in an argument or, as in the two extracts that follow, for bringing things to a striking conclusion.

> . . . what cannot be repaired is not to be regretted. This was obvious; and Rasselas reproached himself that he had not discovered it; having not known or not considered, how many useful hints are obtained by chance, and how often the mind, hurried by her own ardour to distant

views, neglects the truths that lie open before her. He for a few hours regretted this regret . . .

> *The History of Rasselas: Prince of Abyssinia*, Samuel Johnson (1759)

'If you really want to know,' said Mr Shaw with a sly twinkle, 'I think that he who was so willing and able to prove that what was, was not, would be equally willing to make a case for thinking that what was not, was, if it suited his purpose.' Ernest was very much taken aback.

> *The Way of All Flesh*, Samuel Butler (1903)

The breaks between sentences give time for thought. Rudolph Flesch (1962), in *The Art of Plain Talk*, grades writing, according to average sentence length, as very easy to read (less than 10 words), not so easy (10 to 20 words), difficult (20 to 30 words) and very difficult (more than 30 words). You may accept this as a guide, and match your sentence length to the needs of your readers.

Rhythm

Well-written prose has a varied rhythm that contrasts with the strict metered rhythm of verse, and yet contributes to the flow of words in a sentence. With the flow of carefully arranged thoughts in successive sentences, this helps to make a passage interesting and easy to read. Rhythm may give emphasis and help to present shades of meaning.

Use punctuation marks to clarify meaning and to contribute to the smooth flow of language (see chapter 14, *What is the point?*): and always check that your writing is easy to read and sounds well when read aloud. Try not to offend the ear (McCartney, 1953; Phythian, 1985):

1   by unintentional alliteration, as in *rather regularly radial*;
2   by the grating repetition of s, as in *such a sense of success*;
3   by adding s to a word that does not require it (for example, *toward* and *forward*), but the s is correct when these words are used as adverbs (a forward movement; but move forwards) and may be preferred if it makes for easier reading;
4   by the repetition of syllables, as in *appropriate approach*;
5   by the repetition of sound, as in the *thick bark of the cork oak*;
6   by the repetition of cognate forms in different parts of speech, as in a *locality located*, and *except for rare exceptions*; and
7   by repeating a word with a change of meaning, as in a *point to point out*.

Style

Style cannot be added to writing, as a final polish, because it is part of effective prose. Jonathan Swift defined a good style as *proper words in proper places* and Mathew Arnold considered that *the secret of style is to have something to say and to say it as simply as you can.*

In *The Reader Over Your Shoulder*, Graves and Hodge (1947) suggested that prose, although written for silent reading, should sound well when read aloud, and should be consistent in the use of language, without unnecessary ornament, and properly laid out (with each idea in the right place and all connections properly made).

The need for careful planning is also emphasised in George Buffon's address to the Académie française in 1703.

> This plan is not indeed the style, but it is the foundation; it supports the style, directs it, governs its movement, and subjects it to law. Without a plan, the best writer will lose his way. His pen will run on unguided . . . Style is but the order and the movement that one gives to one's thoughts.

A good style depends on the writer's intelligence, imagination and good taste; on sincerity, modesty and careful planning. Rhythm, while not essential, will make for easier reading, and badly constructed sentences may irritate readers and make them less receptive to the writer's message.

How to end

Your conclusion must be decided before you start to write (see page 35) and in a short composition your last paragraph should not normally be a summary (see page 38). Its topic may be the last main point in an argument, upon which you rest your case. Or you may speculate about the future course of events. Just as it is helpful to consider how other writers begin (see page 102), so you can note how others bring their compositions to a close.

However you end, your last paragraph is obviously your conclusion, so do not begin it with the words 'In conclusion . . .'. As the last of an orderly sequence of paragraphs, its first words should follow naturally from the last words of the preceding paragraph. Your conclusion should not take the reader (assessor) completely by surprise. There should be no sting in the tail.

Capture and hold your reader's interest

A novelist, who must capture attention quickly, and maintain interest, takes great care over the choice and use of words. Consider, for example, the first paragraph of a successful novel:

> He rode into our valley in the summer of '89. I was a kid then, barely topping the backboard of father's old chuckwagon. I was on the upper rail of our small corral, soaking in the late afternoon sun, when I saw him far down the road where it swung into the valley from the open plain beyond.
>
> *Shane*, Jack Schaeffer (1954)

The first two words capture attention. The first sentence (in ten short words) tells what the story is about: it begins to answer three of the reader's questions – who, where, and when. The first paragraph makes clear that the story will be told as it affected the life of a small boy. No word is superfluous. Each one plays a part in setting the scene.

Read any newspaper report to see how interest is maintained by reference to familiar things, and by examples, anecdotes and analogies. Harold Evans (1972) in *Newsman's English*, emphasises that:

> Newspapers are short of space and their readers are short of time. The language must be concise, emphatic and to the point. Every word must be understood by the ordinary [reader], every sentence must be clear at a glance, and every story must say something about people.

Newsman's English includes a number of editing exercises in which, by removing superfluous words and rearranging the material, Evans shows how each story can be made more direct and more interesting.

Improve your writing

Write for your readers

1 Decide what your readers need to know (see page 30).
2 In your topic outline underline the points you intend to emphasise.
3 Start with things you expect your readers to know (see page 102).
4 Try to anticipate your readers' difficulties so that you can provide sufficient explanation, an analogy or an example.
5 Keep to the point: do not mislead readers; fulfil their expectations (see page 101).

6　Match your average sentence length to the needs of the readers you have in mind (see page 105).
7　Use punctuation marks to contribute to clarity and to the smooth flow of language (see chapter 14).
8　Remember that too many long words, long sentences and long paragraphs make it harder for the writer to maintain control – and so could make for hard reading.
9　Check that your composition reads well when read aloud.

Make your writing interesting

Approach your readers through their interests rather than your own (see page 107). Remember that people are interested first in themselves and things affecting their nearest and dearest, then in other people, then in animals that live close to people, and then in events as they affect people, their locality, and their country.

To maintain interest, present information at a proper pace. If readers understand they will want to move quickly to the point. However, they must understand every word, every statement and every step in any argument; for if they have to consult a dictionary or read a sentence twice, to confirm that they have taken the right meaning, their attention may be lost.

Use comment words and connecting words (see page 78) to help your readers move smoothly from one thought to the next. Do not direct them away from your explanation or argument by anything irrelevant, by unnecessary detail, by explaining the obvious (but see page 144) or by needless repetition.

When you repeat anything for emphasis or to help clarify a difficult point, use a phrase such as *that is to say* or *in other words* so that the reader knows what you are doing. Otherwise, even after studying both sentences to make sure their meaning is the same, readers may still wonder if they have failed to appreciate some difference.

Write good English

Mistakes in grammar make writing inaccurate, imprecise and ambiguous. Grammar (the art of speaking, reading and writing correctly) is not therefore something that can be ignored. It may be acquired subconsciously by those who speak well and read good prose, or learned with effort from a teacher of English or by studying a textbook on the English language – and reading good prose.

Read good English

In starting to play any game, it is a good idea to watch an expert. Similarly, in learning to write effectively, it is helpful to read good prose.

Evelyn Waugh (see also page 29) advised a young writer to read the works of sixteenth-, seventeenth- and nineteenth-century authors. W. Somerset Maugham, in *The Summing Up* (1938), commends the prose of John Dryden (1631–1700), Joseph Addison (1672–1719), Jonathan Swift (1667–1745), William Hazlitt (1778–1830), John Henry Newman (1801–90), and Matthew Arnold (1822–88). Maugham (see also pages 28–9) considers the two most important qualities in writing to be clarity and simplicity, but regrets that:

> English prose is elaborate rather than simple. It was not always so. Nothing could be more racy, straightforward, and alive than the prose of Shakespeare; . . . To my mind King James's Bible has had a harmful influence . . . There are passages of a simplicity that is deeply moving. But it is an oriental book. Its alien imagery has nothing to do with us. Those hyperboles, those luscious metaphors, are foreign to our genius.

Some of the most successful British and American writers, in every age, have expressed themselves clearly and simply. Francis Bacon (1561–1626) in *Of Studies*, an essay, wrote:

> Read not to contradict and confute, nor to believe and take for granted, nor to find talk and discourse, but to weigh and consider . . . some books are to be read only in parts; others to be read but not curiously; and some few to be read wholly, and with diligence and attention.

In *As You Like It*, written in 1601, William Shakespeare wrote some of the best-known lines in the English language, in words that are still easily understood by all English-speaking people:

> All the world's a stage,
> And all the men and women merely players:
> They have their exits, and their entrances;
> And one man in his time plays many parts,
> His acts being in seven ages. At first . . .

Joseph Addison (1672–1719) in *A Citizen's Diary*, an essay, gave clear advice that is still easy to read and worth considering:

I would, however, recommend to every one of my readers, the keeping a journal of their lives for one week, and setting down punctually their whole series of employment during that space of time. This kind of examination would give them a true state of themselves and incline them to consider seriously what they are about.

In *Robinson Crusoe*, the first English novel, published in 1719, Daniel Defoe wrote one of the best-known passages in English prose. Note the clear, direct and simple style:

One day about noon going towards my boat, I was exceedingly surprised with the print of a man's naked foot on the shore, which was very plain to be seen in the sand. I stood like one thunderstruck, or as if I had seen an apparition.

Thomas Jefferson (1743–1826) wrote The Declaration of Independence of the United States of America, which begins:

When in the Course of human events, it becomes necessary for one people to dissolve the political bands, which have connected them with another, and to assume among the powers of the earth, the separate and equal station to which the Laws of Nature and of Nature's God entitle them, a decent respect to the opinions of mankind requires that they should declare the causes which impel them to the separation.

The continuing appeal of the Declaration is due not only to its expression of the feelings of a people but also to Jefferson's clear and simple style.

William Hazlitt (1778–1830) in an essay *On the Ignorance of the Learned* wrote concisely and gave good advice to students:

It is better to be able neither to read nor write than to be able to do nothing else. . . . Learning is, in too many cases, but a foil to common sense; a substitute for true knowledge. Books are less often made use of as 'spectacles' to look at nature with, than as blinds to keep out its strong light and shifting scenery from weak eyes and indolent dispositions.

Robert Louis Stevenson (1850–94) in *An Apology for Idlers*, an essay, emphasised the need for relaxation and the importance of everyday experiences.

I have attended a good many lectures in my time. I still remember that the spinning of a top is a case of Kinetic Stability. I still remember

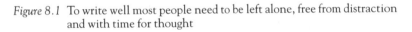

'. . . the print of a man's naked foot . . . in the sand
I stood like one thunderstruck . . .'

Figure 8.1   To write well most people need to be left alone, free from distraction
and with time for thought

that Emphyteusis is not a disease, nor Stillicide a crime. But though I
would not willingly part with such scraps of science, *I* do not set the
same store by them as by certain other odds and ends that I came by in
the open street.

Sir Arthur Bryant wrote a weekly Note Book in the *Illustrated London News*
for more than thirty years. He wrote in clear and simple English; and in *The
Lion and the Unicorn* (1969) he emphasised that the successful author must
capture the reader's interest.

If anyone wonders why my column in the *Illustrated London News* has
any readers, I can only suggest the answer King Charles II gave when
asked to explain how a particularly stupid clergyman, whom he had
made a bishop, had converted his flock from dissent to orthodoxy: 'I
suppose his sort of nonsense suits their sort of nonsense!'

Young writers, still developing a style of their own, will find clear, simple
and straightforward prose in, for example, books by Samuel Butler (see

page 105), Winston Churchill (see page 77), Robert Graves (see pages 17 and 106), George Orwell (see pages 71 and 77), Dorothy L. Sayers (see page 3), and H. G. Wells (see page 17).

Without effort, if you read for pleasure, you will find that your writing improves. Read widely, and you will find that successful authors do not waste words.

> Mr Stevens sat with his map on his knees, because he liked to pick out the distant church spires and name the clustering houses. He liked to find on the map the streams he would cross before they came in sight. He was fond of maps, and had learnt to read them well. They appealed to him because of the endless pleasure they offered his imagination, the picture they showed him of a country built up through the romantic casualness of centuries.
>
> *The Fortnight in September*, R. C. Sherriff (1931)

Just as the way we speak is influenced by the speech we hear, so our writing is influenced by the prose we read. King James's Bible had a profound effect on speech and writing when it was the staple literature of many English-speaking people, just as daily newspapers do now. Most people read newspapers, and some read nothing else. Journalists and broadcasters use the English of today and may have an untold influence on the development of our language.

Read good newspapers

Readers of newspapers look first for things that are of interest; and they read only things that they can understand. Different newspapers are written to appeal to people with different views on politics; or to convert readers to a particular point of view. They are also intended to be understood by people who differ in their reading ability Look carefully at different newspapers to see if you can detect their political bias. In newspapers that you think are for better-educated readers what do you notice about the length of paragraphs, sentences, and words in comparison with those in papers written for less well-educated readers?

Because your vocabulary and style of writing are influenced by the things you read, it is best to read good newspapers. Study the technique of journalists who write well, in feature articles and in leading articles especially, to see how to capture your readers' attention, how to inform, how to express a point of view, how to persuade, how to match your writing to the needs of your readers, and how to write clear, concise, vigorous and vivid prose.

However, it is a mistake to try to copy someone else's style. There is no one correct way to write, because the way you put words together to convey meaning reflects your personality and feeling for words.

Leonard was trying to form his style on Ruskin: he understood him to be the greatest master of English Prose. He read forward steadily, occasionally making a few notes.

'Let us consider a little each of these characters in succession, and first (for of the shafts enough has been said already), what is very peculiar to this church – its luminousness.'

Was there anything to be learnt from this fine sentence? Could he adapt it to the needs of daily life? Could he introduce it, with modifications, when he next wrote a letter to his brother, the lay reader? For example:

'Let us consider a little each of these characters in succession, and first (for of the absence of ventilation enough has been said already), what is very peculiar to this flat – its obscurity.'

Something told him that the modification would not do, and that something, had he known it, was the spirit of English Prose. 'My flat is dark as well as stuffy.' Those were the words for him.

Howards End, E. M. Forster (1910)

9 Finding and using information

Think before you read

Much of what you know comes from personal observation, using your five senses; and you constantly relate new observations to your previous experience. So, whatever you have to write, first make sure that you understand exactly what is required: as indicated by the title of your composition, or the question you must answer, or the terms of reference for any report you are asked to prepare.

Then consider what you already know about the subject. As an aid to thinking, ask yourself the questions any reader of your composition would ask (see page 33). Get as far as you can, preparing your topic outline, before looking at other sources of information (see Table 9.1). This will enable you: (a) to make an original approach to the subject of your composition, and (b) to list the topics (key words) about which you require further information. Then you will be able (c) to concentrate on finding just this information, using the key words when searching contents pages, indexes and databases, and (d) to integrate information derived from different sources as you (e) present the results of your own thinking about the subject – in your own way – in an original composition.

However, remember that the time you spend on the search for additional information must be carefully related to the total time you are able to devote to thinking about, planning, writing, and revising your composition (see Figures 11.1 and 11.2).

The following observations on the importance of knowing what resources are available in a library, and how best to use them, are from an address on reading by John Lubbock, delivered in Manchester in 1903:

> No one can read a good and interesting book for an hour without being better for it; happier and better, not merely for the moment, but the memory remains . . . It is indeed most important that those who

Table 9.1 Some sources of information

Activities	Sources
Thinking	Personal observations
	Private records (notes made in class and during private study)
Talking	Questioning and discussing
	Unpublished records (stored in libraries and elsewhere)
Writing	Correspondence
Reading	Dictionaries
	Encyclopaedias
	Handbooks and standards
	Directories
	Books
	Journals and magazines
	Conference proceedings
	Theses and dissertations
	Newspapers
	Photographs
	Maps
	Audio-visual materials
	Computer-based learning materials
	Computer-based information retrieval systems
	Interactive multimedia resources
	The Internet

use a library should use it wisely. Do we make the most of our opportunities? It is a great mistake to imagine that everyone knows how to read. On the contrary, I should say few do so. Two things have to be considered: what to read and how to read.

What to read

When working at a computer terminal, you may think it easiest to search for information using computer-based retrieval systems. Information technology (the electronic cataloguing, communicating, processing, storing, retrieving, and publishing of information) makes so much information available on a computer or television screen that some students make insufficient use of other sources that are even more readily available in specialist teaching rooms and laboratories, and in libraries (see Table 9.1).

Most of the materials available to you in your college or university library, for example, have been selected by your lecturers and tutors for their usefulness to their students. Furthermore, most of the information available to you in a good library, from books and from other materials, will be either unavailable or not be as readily available elsewhere. So it is important for you to become familiar with the resources available in local libraries, and to consider how best to use them.

Make good use of local libraries

Ask a librarian for help if you have difficulty in finding information on any subject in any library. Ask also if you need advice on, for example, how to reserve books that have been borrowed by other readers, or how to obtain on inter-library loan any books that are unavailable locally.

If you are not sure what information you need, or where to begin your reading, see a lecturer or tutor who teaches the subject and ask for advice. But first, familiarise yourself with the layout of your college or university library and the kinds of learning resources provided for your use.

Dictionaries

A good dictionary of the English language is an essential reference book. It is much more than a guide to correct spelling. Refer to your dictionary whenever you are unsure of the correct spelling, pronunciation or meaning of any word. You will also find information about the origin of each word listed, its function (see Table 14.1), and its status in the language (standard English, colloquial English or slang, see page 71). Using the spell checker of your computer is not an alternative to consulting a dictionary.

Some desk dictionaries suitable for students' use are listed on page 209. For anyone who needs more information than can be included in a desk dictionary, the *Oxford English Dictionary* is a printed multi-volume work with CD-ROM and online versions that provide access from a computer terminal to a database comprising more than 500 000 words.

Other dictionaries that you may find useful are those that provide information about the specialist terms used in the subjects you are studying: but consult your course textbooks first for such information because they are likely to be more authoritative than a dictionary (which covers a wider field) and will include the words in context, with more detail and more explanation than can be provided in a dictionary. There may also be times when you need to refer to a dictionary of abbreviations (see page 65) or of idiomatic expressions (see Table 6.1).

Encyclopaedias

An encyclopaedia is a good starting point for anyone coming new to a subject. Well-known and authoritative encyclopaedias include the single volume *Hutchinson's Encyclopaedia*, the multi-volume *Encyclopaedia Britannica* (also available as a multimedia version on CD-ROM), and *Encarta* (a multimedia encyclopaedia on CD-ROM). As well as such general works, which provide an introduction to most subjects, there are many specialist encyclopaedias – each concerned with one subject or with closely related subjects (for example, the single volume McGraw Hill *Concise Encyclopaedia of Science and Technology*, and the online McGraw Hill *Multimedia Encyclopaedia of Science and Technology*). The multimedia publications include speech and other sounds as well as printed text, and moving pictures as well as stills.

The entries in a printed encyclopaedia are in alphabetical order. Each entry is a concise article, by an acknowledged authority, in language that can be understood by non-specialists – and it ends with references to other sources of further information for those who need to know more. Also, if you look up key words in the index of a printed encyclopaedia you may find other articles of immediate interest, as you may by entering key words in computer-aided information retrieval.

Directories

Telephone directories are a useful source of the names and addresses of people, businesses and organisations, as well as their telephone numbers. Other directories provide similar information about, for example, particular trades or professions. Some directories are available in both printed and electronic versions (for example, all the names and telephone numbers in a complete set of the United Kingdom *Phone Book* are also available on-line and as stand-alone or multi-user versions on CD-ROM). Some directories, available only in electronic form, are called listings. Access to up-to-date computer-based sources of information is also available via television and via the internet (see page 123).

Handbooks and standards

Most handbooks, as the name implies, are small reference books. Some, supplied with commercial products, are called technical manuals. Each handbook or manual provides concise information on one subject. For example, most publishing houses provide a style guide for use by their editors and authors; and some of these guides, including *Copy Editing: The Cambridge Handbook for Editors, Authors and Publishers* (for British English) and *The Chicago Manual of Style* (for American English) are published and widely used as concise guides to an acceptable style of standard written English and to current usage.

Some handbooks, as a result of the addition of more information in successive editions, have become voluminous. For example, *The Handbook of Chemistry and Physics 78th edition 1997–8* (Lide, 1997, New York, CRC Press), which includes tables of data and definitions of scientific terms used in chemistry, physics and related disciplines, has more than 2000 pages.

Standards, produced by national and international organisations in an attempt to promote uniformity in the way things are done, also provide concise information on one subject. For example, standards published by the American National Standards Institution (ANSI), British Standards Institution (BS) and International Standards Organisation (ISO), available in printed and CD-ROM versions (and also via the internet), are listed here in alphabetical order by subject. However, note that standards are revised from time to time – so check that you have the latest version if you need up-to-date information or instructions.

Abbreviation of title words and titles of publications BS 4148 (or ISO 4)

Abbreviations for use on drawings and in text ANSI/ASME Y14.38

Abstracts: guidelines for writing ANSI/NISO Z39.14

Alphabetical arrangement (and the filing order of numbers and symbols) BS 1749

Bibliographic references BS 16290 (similar to ISO 690; more detailed than BS 5605)

Citing and referencing published material BS 5605 (a concise introduction)

Copy preparation and proof correction, Marks for BS 5261C and, for mathematical copy, BS 5261–3 (or see *Proof correction, Marks for, and copy preparation* ANSI Z39.22)

Indexes: content, organisation and presentation BS ISO 999 (also ANSI/NISO TR-02)

Indexes: selection of index terms BS 6529 (similar to ISO 5963)

International System of Units (SI units) BS 5555 (or ISO 1000)

Numbering divisions and sub-classes of written documents BS 5848

Presentation of research and development reports BS 4811

Proof correction, Marks for, and copy preparation ANSI Z39.22 (or see *Copy preparation and proof correction, Marks for* BS 5261C)

References to published materials (including bibliographic and cartographic materials, computer software and databases) BS 1629 (similar to ISO 690)

Scientific and technical reports: elements, organisation and design ANSI/NISO Z39.18

Scientific papers for written and oral presentation, Preparation of ANSI Z39.16

Typescript copy preparation, for printing BS 5261–1

Table 9.2 Three systems used for classifying books in libraries

Dewey decimal system		Universal decimal system	Library of Congress system*
000	General works	0	A
	Reference books (030)	03	AE
100	Philosophy	1	B
	Psychology (150)	15	BF
200	Religion	2	BL
300	Social sciences	3	H
400	Languages	4	P
500	Pure sciences	5	Q
600	Applied sciences	6	
700	The arts	7	N
800	Literature	8	P
900	Geography (910)	91	G
	Biography	92	CT
	History	93	C

Note
* Other classes in the Library of Congress system are K = Law, L = Education, R = Medicine, S = Agriculture, T – Technology and Z = Bibliography.

Books

You might expect all the books a library stocks on any subject to be shelved together in one place, so that readers can see which books are readily available to them. But because many books are of interest to students of more than one subject, a librarian has to decide where each book is best placed. For example, some books on fungi will be shelved with other books on biology or botany, but others may be with books on agriculture, medicine, brewing, timber decay, or stored products – depending on their titles and contents.

In classifying books according to subject, different libraries use different classification systems. So it is worth devoting time to finding out how books and other study materials are classified in the libraries you use. In the Dewey Decimal System, for example, there are ten classes, numbered 000 to 900, with ten divisions in each class (see Table 9.2). Then books are further classified within each division; and the full classification number of each book is written on its spine.

To find books that may be of use to you in a library, or to find a particular book, you must know how to use the library's catalogues. In some libraries the entry for each book is on a separate index card and the cards are filed in drawers. In other libraries the catalogues are on microfiche. But most large libraries have electronic catalogues accessed from computer terminals (which may also be linked via a network to the catalogues of other libraries). However, because both time and money are needed to transfer entries from cards or microfiche to a computer database, some libraries have more than one kind of catalogue (on index cards, on microfiche and electronic).

In card index or microfiche catalogues books are listed both alphabetically (according to the names of their authors or editors, or the organisations that produced them) and by their subject classification.

To access a computer-based catalogue, read any instructions displayed next to the terminal; and then follow the further instructions displayed on the screen. If you know which book you require, you can search by entering its title or the name of an originator (an author, an editor or an organisation). If you need information on a topic but do not have the title or other bibliographic details of a particular book, you can search *either* by entering one or more key words (words you would choose when consulting an encyclopaedia *or* when using the index of any relevant publication) or by entering a subject class number (see Table 9.2). But remember that a keyword search (see also page 122) will help you to find only those books that have the key words you chose in their titles, whereas a subject search should provide you with a list of all titles on the subject that are stocked by the library.

When you find an entry for a book in any library catalogue it will include: the book's bibliographic details and its classification number (its shelf and book number), the number of copies in stock, and a statement as to whether the book is to be used only in the library or can be borrowed. In a catalogue accessed from a computer terminal, if the book is on loan you will also be able to see when it is due to be returned.

Signs on the library's floor plans and on the shelves include both the names of subjects and their classification numbers or letters, as in Table 9.2, to direct readers to the parts of the library in which books on the different subjects are shelved. On each shelf, books on a particular aspect of a subject – with similar book numbers – are arranged in alphabetical order according to the name of the author, editor or other originator. This helps you to find a particular book quickly, and helps you or a librarian to return the book to the same place. It follows from this that if any book has been put on the wrong shelf or in the wrong place on a shelf it may be impossible for anyone to find it. So it is better to leave a book on the table where you have been working, so that a librarian can shelve it correctly, than to return it yourself to the wrong place. This is one reason why in some libraries readers are asked to return all the books they consult to the issue desk – not to the shelves – even if they have used them only in the library.

Reviews

Some books and journals specialise in the publication of articles reviewing the literature on a particular subject, and some reviews are published in journals that also publish original papers. A review of relevant published work is a good starting point in a literature survey, but in a review – as in a textbook – each reference to previous work is necessarily brief and may be misleading.

The only way to be sure that in referring to the work of other writers you do not misrepresent them is to look at their original articles.

Journals, magazines and newspapers

Original articles and up-to-date reviews are published in journals and magazines; and in some subjects newspapers are an important source of information. Your lecturers and tutors are in the best position to say which of the periodicals stocked by your library are likely to be of interest to you, so that you can look at current issues to see if any articles are of interest. Recent issues will probably be displayed in the reference section of your library or in a separate periodicals room, with back numbers less readily available in store.

Academic and trade journals specialise, respectively, in the publication of original research papers and articles about recent developments. Original research papers are called *primary sources*: they contain information that has not been published previously elsewhere. In these you can read the results of recent work soon after it is published, and see references to earlier work that may be of interest. Most articles in other journals, magazines and newspapers, like books and review publications, bring together information that has been published elsewhere, perhaps with new interpretations and new conclusions, and are called *secondary sources*. If you are looking for an article in a journal and do not know in which issue it was published, remember that many journals include an index at the end of each volume.

Many thousands of periodicals are published each year but most libraries can subscribe to only a few (which may be catalogued with all the other materials stocked or listed in a separate periodicals' catalogue); and articles are not necessarily published in what may seem to be the most appropriate journal. As a result, you will miss many articles that could be of interest if you look only at the periodicals stocked by your local libraries.

However, computer-based information retrieval systems provide easy access to articles published in both current issues and back numbers of many journals (see Table 9.3). A search for articles of interest to you can be based on authors' names or on key words (words that you would expect to

Table 9.3 Some electronic sources of information on articles published in journals

Electronic sources*	Access to
America: history and life	Information from books, reviews, media and journals
Analytical abstracts	Chemistry and analytical chemistry
Art abstracts	Art, history of art, museums, photography, films
Biosis	Biology, medicine, microbiology, veterinary science
EBSCO Business Source Elite	Business, marketing, management and economics journals
Emerald	Articles from marketing and management journals
FT McCarthy	Company, industry and market information
Geobase	Earth science, ecology, geography and marine science
Historical abstracts	World history (excluding USA and Canada)
INSPEC	Computing, electrical and electronic engineering and information technology
PubMed	Medicine, life sciences and psychology
Philosopher's index	Books and journals on philosophy
PsycINFO	Psychology and related subjects
Sociological abstracts	Sociology and related subjects
Web of knowledge	Science Citation Index, Social Science Citation Index and Arts and Humanities Citation Index
Zetoc	British Library's Electronic Table of Contents (to about 20 000 journals and 16 000 conference proceedings)

Note
* As with other businesses and organisations, the names, ownership and location of electronic sources may change.

be included in the titles of articles or in journal indexes). You can refine your search, for example, by limiting it to English-language journals or by excluding papers read at conferences. For each article listed as a result of your search you will find the title, the name(s) of the author(s) and other bibliographic details, and either an abstract of the article or the full text.

Another way to refine your search when entering key words is to use the operators *and*, *or* and *not*. For example, if you enter plums *and* custard you will find only those articles that contain both key words; if you enter plums *or* custard you will find all references in the publications searched to either plums or custard separately and to both plums and custard; and if you enter plums *not* custard you will find only those in which plums alone are mentioned, not those in which both plums and custard are mentioned. So care is needed in your use of these operators.

Many journals that publish original and review articles (and many that publish abstracts, lists of contents of current journals, and indexes of key words) are available in electronic versions as well as in print, and some only in electronic versions accessed direct via the internet.

Use resources available via the internet

With a web browser, from a personal computer you can use the web address of a business or other organisation to access its web site and see the pages it provides – which include, for example, words, pictures, videos, plans and maps. Via the internet, therefore, much useful information is available – but also much unsupported opinion, and much that is fiction.

Unlike the papers published in professional journals (in printed or electronic versions), much of the material on web pages has not been subject to peer review and editing. Also, the contents of web pages may be changed at any time, so other people whom you refer to the same source may not be able to read an identical document. Keep these reservations in mind when you use the internet. Also, because web pages may change at any time, you are advised to either make a hard copy or download to your computer any document that is of particular interest.

Many organisations include a web address on their headed notepaper and in advertisements, and there are directories of web addresses, but if you do not know an address you can try to guess it – because most web addresses comprise: www (World Wide Web), the name of the organisation (for example ons = Office of National Statistics), an extension indicating the type of organisation (for example com = company; gov = government), and, except for the USA, the country (for example uk = United Kingdom) with full stops where there are commas in this sentence but with no spaces. For example, www.ons.gov.uk is the web address of the Office of National Statistics, a government department in the United Kingdom. Web addresses can also be located using search engines of an internet service provider (ISP): for example, Google at http://www.google.com. However, when you access a web address you must check that the site is that of the organisation you are seeking – because different organisations, perhaps with opposing objectives, may have very similar addresses.

Via the internet you can also, for example: (a) study previously inaccessible archives, (b) browse through the catalogues of major libraries, (c) scan pages of both current issues and back numbers of newspapers, (d) search indexes for bibliographic details and abstracts of publications likely to be of interest to you (see Table 9.3), and (e) read articles from journals published electronically (which, if necessary, you can print out or down-load to your computer.

Literature Online (LION) is an electronic database of works of English and American literature that can be searched, for example, by author, title or key word. And if you need to know whether or not a book you require is in print, or whether or not the copy you have is the latest edition, you can find full bibliographic details of any book that is in print via the internet by entering its title or the author's name (for example, via Copac at http://www.copac.ac.uk, which provides access to the merged online catalogues of major research libraries in the UK and Ireland plus those of both the British Library and the National Library of Scotland; or via WorldCat, which may be accessed either direct at http://www.oclc.org/worldcat/open/default.htm) or via Google).

The internet also makes available on-line instruction. For example, many of the course materials produced in England by The Open University are available via the internet, with tutorial support, to students in many other countries in western Europe. Similar materials, some based on Open University courses, are available in other countries.

Many people have internet accounts with an ISP and pay for this either by a direct charge or through a telephone company. Anyone with a personal computer making much use of the internet will find this expensive, because a search for information can take a long time. You pay directly because of the cost of the service, and indirectly if you value your time. Also: (a) your search will not necessarily be successful, and (b) you may not be able to rely on relevant material you do find, much of which is likely to be opinion – unsupported by evidence. As when reading books and review articles (secondary sources) you will need to refer to primary sources (see page 121) for the evidence upon which statements are based.

Many of the search engines used in looking for information on the internet offer both a simple search and a more complex search that may be called an advanced search. However, no search engine could search the whole internet, and if you enter identical search requests into different search engines you will find differences in their outputs even when searching for specialist terms. One reason for these differences is that organisations developing web pages use many different key words, not just the most appropriate words, in an attempt to direct searches to their pages. Another reason is that some search engines accept new web pages before others, and some store pages for longer than others.

An intranet (a web similar to the internet but with restricted access) may be available, for example, within a university – linking computers in different rooms, different buildings and different sites. In an international organisation an intranet may link computers in different parts of the world. Because access to an intranet is restricted, the information displayed is easier to control and is likely to be of better quality than much of the information available on the internet.

Use other resources available in libraries

Other sources of information and ideas include maps, photographs, tapes and slides, videos and films. These may be kept in a visual aids section or with books on the shelves of a library, or they may be available in map rooms or other teaching rooms.

If a library's catalogues are computer-based, the non-book materials available in the library will probably be included on the database. Also, a librarian will be able to offer advice on open learning and computer-based learning materials.

How to read

Evaluate each source of information

When you find a book, an article in a journal, or a web page that you think may include information relevant to your current or later needs, consider whether or not it is suitable for your use.

Can you rely on the accuracy of the information included?

The publishers of books for students, or for use in the professions, try to ensure that their books are reliable sources of information. Similarly, editors of learned journals ensure that all articles are checked and approved by academic referees prior to publication. But students using the internet must distinguish for themselves between web pages provided by well-known organisations, which are likely to display useful information, and those that are ephemeral, have not been subjected to peer review, and are unlikely to be worth serious study. Unfortunately, much of the information available on web pages is biased, unsupported opinion. Much is advertising. Much is propaganda.

Is the information included sufficiently up-to-date?

When you open a book, for example, look at the date of publication, printed on the reverse of the title page. Look also to see when the book was reprinted or revised. Minor corrections may be made when a book is reprinted but a new edition normally indicates an extensive revision. Always consider how up-to-date a book is before you read further: you will have to refer to other sources, as well or instead, if you require more recent information or ideas.

Is the publication intended for readers with special interests similar to your own?

In an academic journal the title of an article, with the author's name and affiliations, tells you much about the author's interests and experience; as do the title and preface of a book and the references listed at the end. By reading the headings and sub-headings in an article, or the preface and contents pages of a book, you can get a quick impression of the scope of a work and decide whether or not it is likely to provide the information you need at a level appropriate for your course of study.

Read to find just the information you need at the time

When you have decided to make use of a source of information, remember that an effort is required of the reader as well as of the writer. Read carefully to make sure you take the intended meaning. Read critically as a stimulus to thinking (see *Read critically*, page 26). If possible, obtain information from more than one source. This will help you to see the subject from more than one point of view.

However, remember that what you read is not necessarily true. You may read because you would like to know the facts of the matter but the more you read the more you will find that experts disagree, and the more you will recognise that the opinions of authorities are not to be mistaken for facts. Read critically, therefore: consider the evidence and arguments presented and try to distinguish facts from opinions, and accurate observations from the writer's interpretations.

When reading a book for relaxation and recreation you begin on page one and read every word – perhaps at one sitting. But in study you read for a different purpose. This may be, for example, to learn more about your subject (for background information and ideas), to see how other people organise and present their thoughts (to improve your own communication skills), or in search of information on specific points (to fill gaps in your knowledge and understanding). So do not be put off when you receive long reading lists from lecturers and tutors. You do not need to read the whole of every book you consult (see Figure 9.1).

Some books are written as reference books but even those that can be read as a whole can also be read in part. When you pick up a book, because its title has captured your interest, look at the preface to see the author's intentions. Get into the habit of skim reading to find just the information you need at the time, if this is not clear from the contents pages, or look up key words in the index. You may need to read just one chapter, just one paragraph, or just one sentence. This is a good way to start reading about a

Lost in words

Figure 9.1 The time spent in searching for information must be carefully related to the time available for the work

subject, because you will remember best those things you find of most immediate interest. This way you will also handle more books than would otherwise be possible, and will decide which you might want to use again.

Make good notes as you read

Do not waste time copying long passages from your textbooks or making detailed notes. If you are in the habit of making copious notes, consider whether or not your time could be better spent. Also, remember that if your notes are voluminous they may be too long for use when you are revising for an examination. Instead, learn in two ways: make good use of the textbooks for each part of your course, reading relevant chapters several times if necessary, and make concise notes when you refer to other sources of information.

Many of the books you read are not your own, so you should not mark them in any way. Furthermore, any marks you make in your own books will probably be distracting later when you seek information for other purposes.

Table 9.4 How to record complete bibliographic details of a book

---

Author's or editor's surname and initials (or name of issuing organisation if no author or editor is named).

Year of publication in parenthesis (here or later, see below, depending on house rules).

Title of book (underlined in handwriting and printed in italics, like the names of all publications), with initial capitals used for most words as on the book's title page, and with no quotation marks.

The edition number (except for the first edition).

The number of volumes (e.g. 2 vols) or the volume number (in arabic numerals, underlined with a wavy line in the typescript and printed in bold) but without the abbreviation vol.

The place of publication followed by the name of the publisher, or vice versa, and the year of publication if this has not already been included.

Either the number of the page (p.) or pages (pp.) referred to, or the number of pages in the book (pp.) including preliminary pages (those before page 1).

Example
Gash, S. (1989) *Effective Literature Searching for Students*, Aldershot, Gower.

For more examples, see *References* (page 209).

Authors may present information using words, numbers (usually in tables), or illustrations (diagrams, drawings and photographs), but information presented in one way should not be repeated in another. In reading, therefore, you must study the tables and illustrations as well as the text.

Unless you intend to read the whole of any book, decide what information you require and then turn immediately to relevant pages. Make notes on wide-lined A4 paper (as used for your lecture notes, see page 14). Begin, as when making other notes (see page 16) by recording the date; then record the bibliographic details of the publication (see Tables 9.4 and 9.5).

You must be consistent in the way you record such complete bibliographic details, which you will need if you are to consult the same work again, cite it in one of your own compositions, or include it in a bibliography or list of references.

You are also advised to record the name of the library from which you obtained the publication, and the publication's shelf number, immediately after the bibliographic details. Then, as you make notes, record in the left-hand margin the number of each page from which you make notes. This will save you time if you need to (a) find the same pages again or (b) include page numbers immediately after the publication dates when citing the sources of your information (see page 133).

Table 9.5 How to record complete bibliographic details of an article in a serial publication (a journal, magazine or newspaper)

Author's surname and initials.

Year of publication in parenthesis.

Title of paper, which should not be underlined or printed in italics, with capitals used only for words that would require them in any sentence.

The name of publication (underlined in the typescript and printed in italics, like the names of all publications), with capital letters as on the publication's title page, and with no quotation marks.

The volume number (underlined with a wavy line in typescript and printed in bold) without the abbreviation vol.

The issue number (in parenthesis), or the date of issue.

The first and last pages of the article, joined by a dash.

Examples
DeLacey, G., Record, C. and Wade, J. (1985) How accurate are quotations and references in medical journals? *British Medical Journal* **291** (5499) 884–6.

Horowitz, R. B. and Barchilon, M. G. (1994) Stylistic guidelines for e-mail, *IEEE Transactions on Professional Communication*, * (4) 207–12.

For more examples, see page 118 (BS 16200 *Bibliographic references*, or ISO 690).

When recording the source of information from an internet site, note the name of the originator (author, editor or organisation), the date and title (as for a book, see Table 9.4), followed by the word [online] in square brackets, the place of publication, the publisher (if known), the word Available, and then the name of the internet service provider, an internet address, and [the date accessed] in square brackets (for examples, see page 134).

When recording bibliographic details of a book or of an article published in a journal that is also available on the internet, include the usual reference details (as in Tables 9.4 and 9.5) followed by the medium, for example, [online] in square brackets, then a full stop, the word Available, details of the internet site, and [the date accessed] in square brackets.

If you use the name and date method of citing sources (see page 133), it seems sensible to start the bibliographic details of each source included in your bibliography or list of references with the author's name and the date, but you will find that the order in which bibliographic details are arranged is not the same in all publications. What is important, in any composition you write, is: (a) to include complete bibliographic details of each of the publications cited, (b) to be consistent in the order in which you present these details, (c) while a student to obey all instructions included in any notes for guidance provided by your tutor, and (d) when writing for publication to obey all instructions included in your publisher's notes for authors.

All your notes should be concise, but there is no one correct way to make notes. You may use different methods on different occasions, depending on your purpose and the way the information is presented for your considera-tion. The notes you make when planning a composition, to stimulate your own thoughts, may be set out quite differently from those you make when reading a book. Then your notes will probably be arranged in order, similar to the author's topic outline (words, phrases, headings and sub-headings, concise summaries and simple diagrams), but take care to ensure they are accurate. Such notes may be most useful to you when preparing a topic outline for a composition of your own, to remind you of relevant topics and supporting evidence.

Do not waste time copying long passages word for word. If you think you may need to quote from a publication it is best to take a photocopy. If this is impracticable make sure you write every word and punctuation mark exactly as on the page from which you are copying, plus quotation marks to remind you that it is a quotation and to distinguish these thoughts from your own.

If you omit any of the author's words from a quotation, indicate where these words are missing by three stops . . . preceded and followed by a space (as in the quotation on page 3). If you add anything, to express the author's meaning in fewer or different words, put your words between square brack-ets (as on pages 3 and 6) to make clear which words are the author's and which are your own.

If you cannot understand anything you read, or think it may be incor-rect, put a question mark in the left-hand margin of your notes to remind you to consult other sources of information.

If you add your own thoughts, write your initials in the left-hand margin to remind you that these are not the author's words.

Concise notes are an aid to study. Making notes is an aid to concentra-tion and learning, because you have to decide which paragraphs are relevant to your immediate needs, consider the author's words, make sure you under-stand, and decide what, if anything, you need to note. It is best to read selected paragraphs carefully and then make concise notes, in your own words, when you read these paragraphs again. Include numbered headings; use letters (a), (b), etc. for supporting details; underline or use capital letters for words you wish to remember; use arrows to indicate connections; and use tables and simple diagrams to summarise information or ideas.

Good concise notes made as you read are also an aid to revision. It is best if they can be brief notes added to or combined with your lecture notes (see Figure 9.2), so that you have one set of notes on each aspect of your

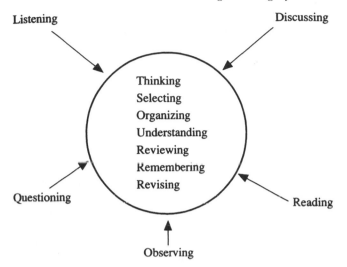

Figure 9.2 The central place of your notes in active study. The different ways in which making notes contributes to learning are included in the circle. The arrows indicate additions to your notes and to your knowledge and understanding from different sources.

work. Indeed, when you feel you have a good grasp of any subject you should consider making even more concise notes. If you prepare such summaries of your notes on index cards, with one card for each topic, these will be most useful to you as revision aids prior to tests and examinations.

You do not have to remember everything that you write but you do need a convenient method of classifying and storing information so that you have immediate access to all your written work. You can use paperclips to hold A4 sheets together, and file the papers dealing with different aspects of your work unfolded in separate A4 (324 × 229 mm) envelopes. Then keep the envelopes concerned with each subject together in a cardboard box (for example, a cereal packet), and keep your index cards in order in a cardboard box (for example, a shoe box). Expensive folders, box files and filing drawers are not necessary.

Improve your writing

Use your notes

When you have to answer a question in coursework do not refer to your notes until you have prepared a first draft of your topic outline (see page 34).

This will help you to produce an original answer – based on *your* knowledge of the subject, on *your* understanding of what is required, and on *your own* ideas as to how this information can best be presented. You can then look at your lecture notes and at other sources of information and, if necessary, revise your topic outline.

Cite sources of information

In your own compositions, never copy complete sentences from books or other sources of information without acknowledging their source. To do so would be plagiarism (stealing someone else's thoughts: see page 24). Like presenting someone else's work as your own, it would be cheating.

One way to draw attention to material quoted from any source is by indentation (as on pages 3–4). Note that the author's name, the date of publication, and the title of the work must all be given (with the title underlined or printed in italics, see page 104), and every word quoted and every punctuation mark must be copied carefully.

If a quotation is included as part of a paragraph, without indentation, quotation marks must be used (see page 17) and the source of the quoted material must be given. However, in scholarly writing it is more usual to summarise information or ideas derived from your reading, in your own words, than to quote another person's exact words. Sources of information must still be clearly stated: (a) so that, as a student, you can demonstrate to an assessor your awareness of relevant sources, and your ability to select relevant material from different sources and integrate this with the information and ideas gained from your own experiences – including class work; (b) to indicate to the reader where further information is to be found; and (c) to acknowledge the work of others (see also *Plagiarism*, page 24).

Even when using your own words, do not cite the source of any published material unless you have read it yourself and are sure that your summary or conclusions do not misrepresent another person's thoughts on the subject.

Two methods of citing sources are widely used in scholarly writing. One, the numeric system, used especially when dealing with old books or papers that include no publication date, is by adding a number after the author's surname or at the end of a statement: in curved (1) or square [1] brackets, or in superscript[1]. For example:

Quiller-Couch (1) listed words that should be used with care by . . .

Quiller-Couch listed . . . by writers who wish to avoid jargon.[1]

A numbered list of sources is then included at the end of the composition, in the order in which they are first cited (see page 118, BS 5605).

In the other method, the name and date system (also known as the Harvard system), the name of the originator of a publication (usually the author of a book or paper, see page 6) is followed by the date on which the book or journal was published. The names of authors are then listed in alphabetical order below the heading *References* (or *Bibliography*, see page 134) at the end of the composition. If two or more works by an author, published in the same year, are cited in a composition, the one cited first is marked by a lower case letter a immediately after the date, the next by a lower case b, etc.

Advantages of this name and date system, for students especially, include the following. (a) You will probably remember the names of authors, and the dates of important publications in your subject, but you cannot remember the complete bibliographic details of every work cited. So, in examinations only the name and date method is practicable. (b) In both coursework and examinations you are writing for tutors and assessors who will recognise many publications from these names and dates and appreciate their relevance without needing to look at your list of references.

When citing a source, using the name and date method, you may write the author's surname, followed by the year of publication in parenthesis, and then write what the author considers or states. Alternatively, you may include a summary of the author's views, findings, or conclusions, and then end your sentence with the author's surname and the year of publication in parenthesis. For example:

> Quiller-Couch (1916) listed words that should be used with care by writers who wish to avoid jargon.

> Words that should be used sparingly and with care, by those who wish to avoid jargon, include case, character and nature (Quiller-Couch, 1916).

Either way, you may be asked to include the relevant page number or numbers immediately after the date, particularly if you quote an author's actual words. For example, you could refer to Quiller-Couch (1916: 77) after the list of words he advised writers to avoid (as on page 72).

In an examination it is not possible to end an answer with a list of references, but you could write the title of a publication, as well as the author's name and the date of publication (as on page 73), to indicate a source of information or ideas.

List your sources of information

End every coursework assignment with a list of all the works you have cited. You should be given credit for having done relevant background reading, as indicated by the sources cited in appropriate parts of your composition: for the understanding made clear in your composition; for your ability to integrate relevant material from different sources; and, if appropriate, for your critical analysis. This is why you should cite sources and list references in every composition, from the start of your course. Do not wait until you have to prepare a longer dissertation, extended essay, term paper or report.

In some subjects, especially the arts and humanities, you may be asked to include complete bibliographic details of each of the works you have consulted while preparing your composition, which have influenced your thinking, even if some are not cited in your composition. Such a list should be headed *Bibliography*.

In other subjects, especially the sciences and engineering, the preferred heading is *References*. For this there are two rules. (a) Cite no publication unless you have had it in your hands and read the whole work or just selected parts, to ensure that you do not misrepresent the author. (b) List complete bibliographic details of every work cited in your composition, but no others, in alphabetical order according to the authors' surnames.

For further guidance on how to list publications that have more than one author, and on how to list different types of publications (for example, a paper in conference proceedings, or a chapter by one author in a book edited by someone else), note how sources are cited and how references are listed in publications recommended for further reading as part of your course of study. See also relevant standards (page 134).

For an online introduction to the name and date method of citing and listing sources, including an introductory video, on-screen instruction, test questions and self-assessment, see: University of Sunderland (2003) *Guide to the Harvard method of citing and listing references* [online]. Available http://www.library.sunderland.ac.uk/findinginformation/help-support/infobites/ [27 October 04]. The home page for this guide is http://www.sunderland.ac.uk

10 Answering questions in tests and examinations

Only you can decide on ways of working that suit you best, but consider the following advice – which should help you to avoid the mistakes made by many students when preparing for and taking tests and examinations.

Early in your course obtain a copy of the course programme so that you have a good idea of the course content. Then look at the list of learning outcomes included in your course guide, or at the published syllabus on which your coursework and examination assessments will be based.

But remember that your only complete guide to the course content, and so to what may be expected in tests and examinations, should be: (a) your own lecture notes, (b) your practical work and other coursework assignments, (c) the lists provided in lectures and tutorials to guide your background reading, and (d) the examination papers set for students taking the course in previous years.

Work steadily throughout your course. Make sure that you understand all aspects of your work as you go along, and that you have a good set of notes (see page 131); and keep up-to-date with all set work – so that you are always in control.

You will be able to obtain copies of the examination papers taken by students on your course in previous years. Look at these to see how the papers are arranged, what choice of questions you can expect in each subject, and what kinds of questions are asked on each paper. Plan answers to questions, as part of your revision. If you are uncertain of the precise meaning of any question, or exactly what is required in the answer, discuss this with a lecturer. Planning answers will help you to concentrate on your studies and will give direction to your work.

Taking tests as part of coursework

You may not be allowed to see copies of the test papers set in previous years, as part of coursework, for students taking your course. But you should, at least, be given examples of the kinds of questions that you may be expected to answer.

Most tests differ from examinations in that they comprise questions that require only short answers. They are useful as part of coursework because they can test your knowledge and understanding of most topics included in the syllabus or in the list of learning objectives for the course. Regular tests serve to remind students that revision is part of active study, and help them to recognise gaps in their knowledge or understanding – and then rectify any weaknesses. Test results also provide feedback to assessors – indicating parts of the course that some students are finding difficult, and helping them to identify particular students who need extra tutorial instruction or guidance.

In some courses tests are used not only to promote learning and to improve teaching but also to provide marks that contribute to the final assessment of each student's performance. This is fair to all students, in that they are all assessed at the same time, answering identical questions, under examination conditions. But like assessments based on homework, if such tests are held during the course they have the disadvantage that students are being tested while they are still learning – before they have had the opportunity to benefit from the course as a whole (see page 7). That is to say, an attempt is being made to assess learning outcomes before it is possible to know the outcomes (before the course is completed). Such tests are, therefore, contrary to the whole spirit of higher education and the encouragement of continuing personal development.

If, to avoid this criticism, such tests are held only at the end of the course they are useful as a method of assessment – and are easier to mark than examinations in which essay-type answers are required – but then they do not contribute to effective teaching and learning – because it is too late for any feedback. Assessors learn, too late, of any student who with help could have scored higher marks; and students, having completed the course, are unlikely to see the assessor again – and so are likely to repeat mistakes that could have been corrected had appropriate feedback been provided earlier in the course.

Answering questions in tests

Revise for each test, as you would for an examination, but use a different technique when taking the test: (a) if each question requires only a short answer, and (b) if you are required to answer every question.

Because only short answers are required, and you may be tested on all aspects of the course, if you have missed even one class you may be unable to answer some questions.

Because you have to answer all the questions, it would be a waste of time to read them all first – as you would if you had to decide which ones to answer and in what order to answer them.

Instead, read the first question. Think about it. If you are sure you understand exactly what is required, and you know the answer, write your answer at once. There may be space on the question paper for your answer. If there is, accept this as an indication of the length of answer expected. Do not try to write more. The number of marks available for a complete and correct answer to the question may also be stated. If it is, this may be an indication of the number of different points you are expected to include in your answer. As you complete your answer, put a tick in the left-hand margin of the question paper next to the question number.

Work through the paper, answering all the questions you know you can answer correctly, but do not spend long puzzling over any question if the answer does not come immediately to mind. Instead of a tick, put a question mark in the margin of the question paper, next to the question number, to remind you to look again at this question if you have time.

In this way you will ensure that you do answer all the questions you feel confident you can answer correctly, whereas if you were to spend too long thinking and worrying about any questions you found difficult you could run out of time and find that you had left some easy questions unanswered.

If you have time, after working through the paper once, go through it again, tackling the questions you have not already answered. You may find, on second thoughts, that you can answer some of them.

If you do not know the answer to any question, and you know that marks will not be deducted for an incorrect answer, you must guess. Just by chance some of your guesses are likely to be correct – and score some marks. In a multiple-choice test, choose the answer you think is most likely to be correct. Because you know something about the subject, your guesses are more likely to be right than wrong.

Sometimes, after a test or examination, you realise that you have not done your best work. Nothing is to be gained by worrying about this. However, if you are allowed to look at your answers after they have been marked, consider the assessor's comments carefully to see if you can learn from them – as you should when coursework is returned to you after marking (see page 49).

Taking examinations

If you have revised regularly throughout your course (see page 135) you should be keyed-up and ready for action – as an athlete would, after months of training, immediately before a race – and should not be over-anxious.

However, the advice in this chapter should help all students to approach examinations with greater confidence.

As a student you should have a desire to learn, but examinations are an additional incentive. Each examination passed provides encouragement and satisfaction, confirming that you have reached a certain standard. However, many students do not do as well as they could in examinations. Some have not worked hard enough and do not know as much about their subjects as they should. Some, although they have worked hard, have not organised their time effectively. And some have worked hard, organised their studies, and know their subjects, yet have not thought enough about examination technique.

You may not be allowed to see your own examination answers, after they have been marked, so you may not be aware of all your own mistakes – relating to your knowledge, your understanding, or your examination technique. Consider, therefore, the faults in examination technique that contribute to the under-achievement of many students.

Learn from other students' mistakes

1 Master your subjects

The most common reason for under-achievement in examinations is inadequate preparation. To master all your subjects, you need to develop your interest in them, keep fit, use your leisure time effectively, concentrate during hours of study, study effectively, develop your ability to communicate effectively, and revise your work regularly throughout your course.

2 Select questions as directed in the instructions at the head of the question paper

Some candidates fail to answer compulsory questions – and can therefore score no marks for them. They cannot make good this omission by answering extra questions from other parts of the paper. Such extra questions will not be marked.

Some candidates when asked, for example, to answer four questions and to answer at least one from each of the sections of the paper A, B and C, answer no questions from one section. They can score no marks, therefore, for this section. And the examiner will mark only three questions from the other sections, even if four have been answered.

3 Select questions carefully

Some candidates do not read the whole paper before deciding which questions to answer.

If an examination paper comprises many questions, each requiring only a short answer, and if all questions are to be answered, then it is probably best to start at the beginning and to work through the paper to the end – as in a test. Each question can be read, understood, considered, and a short answer recorded. Any question that is not answered immediately can be reconsidered later.

However, most advanced examinations are not of this kind. If there is a choice of questions, you must allow a proportion of the time available for reading all the questions carefully. Consider what is required in each answer before deciding which questions you can answer best. If you do not do this, you may find, after the examination, that you could have made a better choice and scored higher marks.

4 Answer the required number of questions

The marks allocated to each question may be stated on the examination paper. If not, assume that the same number of marks will be available for each answer (so that up to 25 marks could be scored for each question if four have to be answered).

If you were to attempt five questions when instructed to answer four, only your first four answers would be marked: no marks could be given for your fifth answer. Time spent answering questions that will not be marked is time wasted: time that should have been used in answering the questions that will be marked.

If you were to attempt only three or two questions, when you should be answering four, you could not receive more than 75 and 50, respectively, of the 100 marks available.

So you must do your best to answer the right number of questions. If you find you cannot do this, consider how best to cope with the situation. If you should answer four questions but can answer only three, work steadily at these three and you could still score high marks (up to 75 out of 100). And if you can answer only two questions you could still pass the examination (with up to 50 out of 100). However, you should be able to score some marks for relevant material when answering questions you feel you cannot answer well, so it is always best to answer the right number of questions – even if to do so your answers to some questions have to be superficial or otherwise incomplete.

5 *Allocate your time according to the marks available*

Some candidates spend too much time on some questions, and so cannot spend enough time on others. They may even find that they have no time for their last answer. Make sure you know how much time is allowed for the whole examination: then divide your time wisely. The instructions at the head of the paper may include advice as to how long you should spend on each part of the paper.

If the marks available for a question (or for the parts of a question) are stated on the paper, next to the question, this also indicates how you should allocate your time.

If the questions carry equal marks try to allocate your time equally between them (see Table 10.1). Resist the temptation to spend more time on the question you feel you can answer best (see Table 10.2). Remember, it is easier to score a few marks by answering a question that you at first felt you did not know much about than it is to score a few extra marks by spending extra time on what is already a good answer.

If you spend 50 minutes on a question that the examiner expects you to answer in 36 minutes, you will probably be including irrelevant material, or padding, or repeating yourself (perhaps using different words), or giving unnecessary detail, extra examples, or more explanation than is needed.

If you find that you are running out of time, towards the end of an examination, it is better (a) to write a good topic outline for a complete answer or to answer a question in note form than (b) to leave one question unanswered or to write only the first part of an answer that you do not have time to complete.

6 *Answer precisely the question asked, not a slightly different question*
that you thought might be asked

Some candidates, during their revision, prepare an answer to a question set in a previous year that they think may be set again. Then they write their prepared answer in the examination – even though the question set is not identical with the one for which they have prepared. That is to say, they fail to respond to the exact wording of the question (see page 32). The result, at best, is that they cannot score full marks. At worst, they may write at length, including some things that would have been relevant had they been presented as an answer to the question set, and yet score no marks.

If you plan an answer during your revision, do read the question set in the examination carefully to ensure you know exactly what is required. Then plan your answer to the question set: include only relevant material, in an appropriate order, as *your* answer to *this* question.

Table 10.1 Allocating your time to examination questions

Duration of examination	Number of questions to be answered	Available for each question	
		Time*	Marks
180 min	6	30 min	17
	5	36	20
	4	45	25
	3	60	33

Note
* Deduct a proportion of the time needed for reading all questions, deciding which questions to answer, and checking your answers, from the time available for answering each question.

Table 10.2 Three ways of allocating your time in a three-hour written examination, and the possible consequences

Question	Time allocation	Marks	Time allocation	Marks	Time allocation	Marks
1	55 min	16	55 min	16*	36 min	14
2	50 min	14	50 min	14	30 min	13
3	40 min	11	40 min	11	36 min	12
4	35 min	11	15 min	8	36 min	11
5	none	0	15 min	6	36 min	10*
Totals		52		55		60

Note
* In a written answer it is difficult to score more than sixteen out of twenty for a good answer, but if you have studied effectively it is relatively easy to score half marks by attending carefully to a question that at first reading you thought you did not know enough about to prepare a good answer

7 Keep to the point

Some candidates, because they do not know the answer or do not read the question carefully enough, write more than is required and yet still do not answer the question set. Perhaps remembering a relevant lecture, or having memorised several pages of notes on the subject, they insist on pouring forth all that they know. Instead they should be giving a considered answer: selecting and arranging only relevant points from their notes – and adding relevant information and ideas from other sources.

If asked to give a reasoned account of the circumstances leading to an event, a student might mention some things that happened before the event, describe the event in detail, and then discuss some after-effects. Yet there could be no marks for the description of the event, or for discussing its consequences, because the question did not ask for these things. And because only some circumstances leading to the event are mentioned, this part of the composition could not be considered well reasoned or complete. In other words, much time might have been spent on this work, and the student might feel pleased at having remembered so much and at covering so many sheets of paper with writing – yet very few marks could be awarded.

8 Answer all parts of the question

When examinations are set the examiners prepare outlines of the answers they expect. Then they allocate marks to the parts of each answer. You are likely to score most marks if, before starting to write, you prepare a plan that includes all the topics in the examiner's marking scheme (preferably in the same order). This is why you must read the question carefully and then think about what is to be included in a complete and balanced answer. You cannot score any of the marks available for the parts of a question that you do not answer.

With a structured question, which indicates clearly the separate parts required in your answer, consider what must be included in each part. Also, use your judgement in deciding how many marks are likely to be available for each part. Then allocate your time accordingly. If you spend too much time on one aspect of your answer you cannot score more than the number of marks allocated to this aspect. If you then spend too little time on other aspects you may not make the best use of your knowledge and so you are likely to score fewer marks than you should. For any aspects that you ignore, you can score no marks. Preparing a topic outline for your answer will help you visualise the examiner's marking scheme. What *exactly* does the examiner want to know?

9 Plan your answers

Some candidates are unwilling to spend time on thinking about questions and planning answers in examinations. There is a temptation to write throughout the examination, and to write as much as possible. This temptation should be resisted. Planning is especially important in examinations, because time is limited. As a result of the time devoted to preparing a topic outline, the remaining time available for answering the question can be used effectively (see Table 10.3).

Without thought and planning, you are unlikely to present information in the most effective order. You will probably include information on one topic in different parts of the answer, include too much detail on some

Table 10.3 Allocating the 30 minutes available for a written answer, when you have to answer six questions of similar length in a three-hour examination

Activity	Time needed (minutes)
Thinking about the question	3
Planning your answer	2
Writing (all the main points with enough explanation)	22
Checking	3

topics and not enough on others, omit essential points, and repeat other points unintentionally. Your answer as a whole is unlikely to be well balanced.

Such disorganised answers give an unfavourable impression of the writer and are difficult to mark. Remember that marks are awarded according to a marking scheme, for relevance, completeness, and understanding. You must therefore decide on a limited number of main points (topics for your paragraphs) that the examiner will expect you to deal with in the limited time available for your answer. Any irrelevant material is likely to be deleted by the examiner. The inclusion of irrelevant material is not only a waste of time but it also serves as a smokescreen – making any relevant material harder to find.

Prepare a plan or topic outline for each answer. You may do this immediately before starting the answer. Alternatively, you may prefer to plan all your answers at the beginning of the examination so that you can reconsider each outline later – immediately before writing your answer.

Planning will help you to remember things; and your topic outline will help you to get started and give direction to your work (see page 140). Furthermore, additional points will come to mind as you write – according to your plan.

You may decide to answer any compulsory questions first. Or you may answer first the questions you feel you can answer best. There are advantages in this, especially if you plan all your answers at the beginning of the examination, because it gives time for second thoughts about other questions. Then you will probably benefit from reconsidering each question before you start to answer it. However, you should take care to spend no more time than you should on what you think are the easy questions (at the start of the examination). If you do, you will have *less time* for the other questions: some of which may need *more thought*.

10   Display your knowledge

Some candidates omit relevant things because they consider them too elementary. However, in examinations you score marks by displaying your knowledge and understanding. Basic facts and ideas should be included, even if briefly and in passing, at appropriate places.

Similarly, in numerical questions the stages in your calculation must be shown. The examiner can then give marks for the part of your work that is correct – even if the answer is wrong. If you simply give the wrong answer you can score no marks.

11   Make clear your understanding

Some candidates include relevant material in their answers, but do not score high marks because they fail to make clear their understanding. In advanced examinations, especially, it is not usually enough simply to demonstrate that you have a good memory. You should show your intelligence by planning each answer so that you can select relevant information and ideas and present them in an effective order.

Show that you understand what is required in each part of your answer by using words from the question at appropriate points in your answer: perhaps you can use them as topic sentences or as sub-headings. Show your understanding in each paragraph by starting with the main point you wish to make in the paragraph (in a direct and forceful topic sentence), by including *enough* evidence or *explanation*, and if appropriate by giving an example.

Use each part of your answer, and each paragraph, as an *opportunity to score marks* by adding only relevant information and ideas, and by making clear your understanding.

12   Cite sources of information

Pay sufficient attention, in your answers, to points emphasised in lectures and other classes – which your lecturers considered important – but as in coursework it is not usual to acknowledge these sources of information. However, you are advised to refer to relevant published work – citing sources as you would in coursework. Examiners will recognise important contributions to their subject by the authors' names and the dates of publication, but you may wish to refer to some books by their titles as well as giving their authors' names. You will not be expected to remember full bibliographic details, so your answers to examination questions should not end with a bibliography or with a list of references cited.

13 Arrange your answer for easy marking

Some candidates give a jumbled answer, making it difficult for the examiner to tell whether or not each part of the question has been answered. Remember that the examiner may have many scripts to mark. Try to make the task as easy as you can – so that it is easy to award the marks you have earned.

The different kinds of question set in coursework and examinations must be tackled in different ways. If a question is set in parts, you are advised to arrange the parts of your answer in the same order as they appear in the question (see page 34). Use letters (a), (b), (c) etc. if these are used in the question. Otherwise, select appropriate words from the question, if you can, as sub-headings. These signposts will help the examiner, allocating marks according to a marking scheme, to find and mark the parts of your answer. They will also help you to ensure that you do answer all parts of the question and allocate your time appropriately to each part.

In other types of questions, clear paragraph breaks should indicate that you have said all that you intend to say about one topic and are just about to start a new topic. By planning you can deal adequately with each topic in one place – and so make it easy for the examiner to award marks.

Do not leave blank pages between your answers, and do not leave gaps within any answer. If you were to leave a gap at the bottom of a page and then continue your answer on the next page, the examiner could award a mark – thinking your answer was finished – only to find additional material on the next page and have to read this before reconsidering the mark.

14 Express your thoughts as clearly as you can

Some candidates use more words than are needed to convey their intended meaning precisely, probably because they do not know much about the subject and are trying to make their limited knowledge go a long way. Perhaps they think that marks are given for the number of pages filled with writing.

On the contrary, words that convey no meaning are like hurdles in a race: they hinder the reader's progress and so make it harder for the writer to convey meaning. Instead of displaying what is known, the extra words obscure meaning and give the immediate impression that little or nothing is known.

Examiners see too much padded writing – full of superfluous words, gobbledegook, surplusage, verbosity – and are unlikely to be impressed by an excess of words. They may be annoyed if they have to search for relevant material, or, being unwilling to search, are more likely to skim read the answer and then give a low mark.

15 *Write for easy reading*

Remember that marks are given for content and quality of your answers – not for their length. Write complete and carefully constructed sentences so that your meaning is clear. Some candidates make mistakes in their choice of words, in spelling, punctuation and grammar, or write a careless scrawl. All these things make for hard reading, and create an immediately unfavourable impression.

Examiners can give marks only for what is written – not for what they think a candidate probably meant. And they can give marks only for what they can read.

16 *Check your answers*

Some candidates complete their last answer just as the instruction is given to stop writing. They leave no time for checking their work.

If at all possible, leave yourself time to read through all your answers. Check that you have answered all parts of each question. Check that every word is legible. Correct any slips of the pen, obvious mistakes, or sentences that do not make sense. Check calculations, including substitutions in formulae, algebraic and arithmetic operations, and the position of each decimal point. Check that the result of any calculation is a reasonable answer to the question you are answering.

By making corrections yourself you can avoid being penalised for the mistakes. You may also score marks by adding important points that you did not remember previously, and without which your answer would have been incomplete.

17 *Use your time effectively*

Concentrate fully: do not allow your mind to wander. If a diagram is needed, do not waste time on unnecessary lines or on shading (see Figure 10.1). Distinguish the parts of a diagram by using coloured pencils for the lines, and by clear labelling (see page 100).

Remember, if you make a mistake or have second thoughts, that the quickest way to delete a number, letter, word or paragraph is to draw one straight line through it. Delete with an oblique line through single letters and with a horizontal line through words, so that you have space for corrections between your lines of writing. Never waste time erasing words with a rubber or with correcting fluid: when hand-writing it is always quicker to delete words with one stroke of a pen.

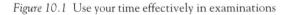

Do not waste time on shading

Figure 10.1 Use your time effectively in examinations

Answering questions in a theory examination

1 *Read and obey all the instructions* printed on the front cover of your answer book. For example, you may be told to use a separate answer book for each part of the paper, to start each question at the top of a page, and not to leave spaces within an answer or blank pages between the end of one answer and the start of the next.

2 *Check that you have been given the correct question paper*, that it is properly printed, and that you have the whole paper.

3 *Read the instructions at the head of the question paper.* Make sure you under-stand how much time you are allowed, how many questions you should answer, and whether or not there are any compulsory questions or any other restrictions on your choice.

4 *Read the whole paper – all the questions – if you have a choice of questions.* Look at both sides of each sheet to make sure that you do see all the questions.

5 *Select the questions that you can answer most fully*, then look again at the instructions at the head of the paper to check that you have selected the right number of questions, and that your selection includes any compulsory questions and will be acceptable to the examiners.

6 *Allocate your time* to planning, writing and checking, so that you can do your best (a) to answer any compulsory questions, (b) to answer the right number of questions, and (c) to answer each question as fully as you are able in the time you have available for that question (see page 141).

7 *Read each question again before you plan your answer.* Consider every word and phrase to ensure that you understand exactly what the examiner wants to know, and that you respond to any instructions as to how your answer is to be presented (see page 32).

8 *Plan your answer.* You cannot afford to spend much time deciding how to begin your answer; but a suitable starting point will probably become apparent as you prepare your topic outline. In the first paragraph you will probably use some words from the question in a context that makes clear to the examiner that you understand the question and have begun your answer. Indeed, your first sentence or paragraph may give the essence of your answer.

9 *Do not waste time copying out the question.* Before answering the question, simply write the number of the question conspicuously in the left-hand margin (as instructed on the front cover of your answer book).

10 *Get to the point quickly and keep to the point.* Work to your topic outline so that you can give an answer that is well balanced and well organised and so that you can make all your main points effectively in the time available – without digression or repetition (see page 41).

11 *Respond to the words used in the question* (see page 67). Do not make vague statements. Give reasons and examples. Include enough explanation.

12 Do not leave things out because you consider them too simple or too obvious. The examiner cannot assume that you know anything. *You can score marks only for what you write.*

13 If you include anything that is not obviously relevant, explain why it is relevant.

14 Use small letters (a), (b), (c), etc., or sub-headings, or distinct para-graph breaks, as appropriate, *to make clear to the examiner* where your answer to one part of the question ends and your answer to the next part begins.

15 If a question is set in several parts, spend enough time on each part of your answer. Also, do your best to answer the parts in the same order as they appear in the question, because *the examiner will prefer to mark them in that order.*

16 If the number of marks allocated to each part of a question is shown on the examination paper (next to each question), *accept this as a guide* (a) to how much time you should devote to each part of your answer and (b) to the number of relevant points needed for an adequate answer to each part.

17 *Make any diagram simple* so that you can complete it quickly and neatly. Use coloured pencils, if necessary, to represent different things, but do not waste time on shading.

Draw each diagram in the most appropriate place (probably where you first mention it in your answer) but number it so that you can refer to it, if necessary, in other parts of your answer.

If diagrams are necessary, they should complement your writing, making explanation easier and enabling you to present information and ideas that you could not present adequately in words alone. Effective diagrams should therefore reduce the number of words needed in your answer. *Do not waste time conveying the information in both words and pictures.*

18 *Write legibly in black or blue-black ink.*
When you have completed your answer, and are sure that all the points you intended to make are included, cross out your topic outline and any rough work so that the examiner can see at once that they are not part of your answer. However, remember that coloured ink may be mistaken for the examiner's corrections. Use *only* black or blue-black ink yourself, unless you need other colours in diagrams.

19 Keep an eye on the time, so that you can spend the right amount of time on each question (see page 141) and have time to check all your answers towards the end of the examination (see page 146).

20 Try to finish each question before starting the next, unless you get as far as you can with a question or are unable to solve a problem. Then be prepared to leave it. You can come back to it after answering the other

questions if you have time. You may well make more progress, after a break, at your second attempt.

21 Do not leave before the end of the examination. If you have checked your work and have time to spare (see Figure 10.1), look again at each question and at the topic outline for your answer. Consider if there is anything you could add to any of your answers, to score extra marks. Check that you have written your name and examination number, and any other information required, on the front cover of your answer book.

Answering questions in a practical examination

Practical work, whether in a laboratory or as part of field work, is one important source of information (see page 16). Relevant personal observations and experiences should be included in your answers to questions in coursework and in theory examinations. However, your knowledge of practical techniques will usually be actually tested in practical exercises as part of coursework, in project work and in practical examinations.

In taking a practical examination the basic rules are similar to those stated for a theory examination.

1 Obey all instructions printed on the front cover of your answer book, and at the head of the question paper.

2 Read all the questions, unless you have to answer every question.

3 If you have a choice, decide which questions to answer.

4 Decide the order in which you will tackle the questions. Even if you are asked to attempt every question, the order that suits you best may not be the order in which the questions are arranged on the paper.

5 Allocate your time, remembering that in practical examinations you may be able to leave one question for a while (for example, to let something develop) and to come back to it later after you have started or completed another task that may be part of another question: just as when preparing a meal it is necessary to work on several tasks at once if all are to be completed – with each course ready to eat – at the right time.

6 Read each question again before starting your answer, and follow any instructions carefully.

7 Spend as much time as is necessary on the questions you find easy – even if few marks are available for each of them. These few marks may help you to make a fail into a pass, or to make a good grade into a better one.

8 Use black or blue-black ink and make sure that your writing is legible.

9 Keep an eye on the time, and allow time to check all your work towards the end of the examination.

10 Do not leave before the end.

11 Writing a dissertation, long essay, term paper, project report or thesis

As part of your course you may have the opportunity to work independently, with a supervisor to offer advice when necessary, on an aspect of your subject that you find of particular interest. Your written account of this special study may be called a *dissertation*: a setting forth of the results of a study of documents, or a review of relevant published work, or both, and including argument, evidence, explanation, and perhaps also description, and leading to some conclusion. A similar composition may be called an *extended essay*, which simply means it is longer than your answers to the questions set as part of other coursework; or a *term paper*, which indicates that more time is allowed for this work than you would need for preparing most coursework assignments.

A *project report* is considered here to differ from a dissertation in that it is based on personal observations or on a survey. It involves the collection of qualitative and quantitative data, the analysis of these original data, the interpretation of the results of this analysis, and a consideration of these results in relation to relevant published work. In these respects it is similar to the composition that forms part of a submission for the award of a higher degree, which is usually called a *thesis*.

Preparing a longer composition is a test of your ability: (a) to demonstrate your knowledge, understanding and critical evaluation of documents or publications; (b) to communicate information and ideas in writing, supported, if appropriate, by tables and diagrams; and (c) to complete the work in a given time.

Different kinds of work will be reported in different ways, and your supervisor will probably provide you with notes for guidance that make clear what is required of all students taking your particular course. To help you further with this composition, consider the advice included in this chapter. Then refer to the *Index* when you need advice on particular points.

Agree your terms of reference with your supervisor

Your supervisor will help you to define the purpose and scope of your special study (so that you know what is required), and will try to ensure that the task is one that you can complete in the time available (without neglecting your other studies and without its interfering with your preparation for examinations). You must not attempt too much (see Figure 11.1).

Before starting, make sure that any essential documents, equipment or other materials will be available when you need them. Check that any essential publications are available in your library or can be obtained from elsewhere when you need them.

Choose a subject in which you are already interested and which will complement and support your other studies. If possible, look at satisfactory reports completed by other students in previous years of your course to get an idea of what they were able to achieve in the time available.

In other coursework, and in examinations, you have to prepare written answers to questions. Each question must be carefully worded so that you know exactly what the assessor requires in your answer. Similarly, in administration, business or research any report is preceded by clearly worded terms of reference. These state the purpose of the work reported and limit its scope.

Your special study will have a concise title, which should either be complete in itself or be followed by a clear statement of your terms of reference. Your supervisor may write both the title and your terms of reference, or you may write them yourself after discussing the scope of the work with your supervisor. But if you write them, you must check that they are acceptable to your supervisor before continuing with your work; after which you must not change either without consulting your supervisor.

Find out how your work will be assessed

Your special study should provide you with more opportunities to display your initiative, ingenuity and originality than does other coursework; and with the opportunity to demonstrate your ability to select relevant material and present this in a way that is appropriate for the intended audience (probably your supervisor, a second internal assessor, and an external examiner).

Your essay or report should therefore indicate, as appropriate, not only what you have done but also your approach to the problems involved, to the interpretation of work done by others, and to the analysis and interpretation of any new observations. Because of all these things, as in all coursework, what you write and how you write will play a major part in the assessment of your work.

Project reports are assessed, not weighed

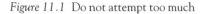

Figure 11.1 Do not attempt too much

It is difficult for an examiner to arrive at an objective assessment of project work. This is particularly true for an external examiner who has not previously been associated with the work in any way. Unless there is an oral examination, the written account is the external examiner's only guide to the quality of the work.

However, it may be difficult for any assessor to decide how much of the report is the student's own work. All students need help in limiting the scope of their special study, but once this has been agreed the supervisor should ensure that the student has clear terms of reference in writing so that there is no possibility of misunderstandings later. The supervisor should also try to ensure that the work begins well, and should monitor progress regularly – offering help when this is obviously needed, and when it is requested. Students should also be encouraged to ask other people for information or advice. Then any technical assistance received should be acknowledged (see page 156), as should all published sources of information (see page 132). Obviously, you must not present other people's thoughts as if they were your own or other people's work as your own (see *Originality*, page 23).

Inevitably, some special studies provide more opportunities than do others for students to show initiative, ingenuity and originality; and different students have different supervisors. These differences, which make objective assessment difficult, must be considered carefully if all students are to be treated as fairly as possible.

There is probably no one correct solution to these problems but it is possible to list criteria that should influence the final assessment. These cannot all be judged at the end of the work.

1 The student's ability to define clearly the problem to be tackled or the purpose of the work, if the subject was chosen by the student.

2 The thoroughness with which the work was tackled in relation to the time available, and the planning of the work.

3 The accuracy with which information is recorded.

4 The student's ability to evaluate published work, to make original observations, to record and analyse data (as appropriate), to argue logically, and to draw valid conclusions.

5 The student's ability to relate personal observations and findings to the published work of others.

6 The student's ability to select relevant material, reject what is irrelevant, and convey the results of this special study in a well-written composition. A good student will write a clear, concise, considered, critical, balanced, well-organised and well-presented dissertation or report. In contrast, an incomplete, opinionated, superficial or uncritical composition, with inadequate reference to relevant sources of information, will be recognised as lacking rigour.

These six aspects of the work might be considered of comparable importance and be given equal weight in a marking scheme. But, whatever method of assessment is adopted, each student needs to know, before starting a special study, how the work is to be reported and how the exercise as a whole will be assessed.

Organise your work

Irrespective of the subject of your special study, it will involve many weeks' work and your written account will probably be longer and more demanding than anything you have written previously. It must be carefully planned so that each aspect of the work can be reported in the most appropriate part of your composition.

Table 11.1 The parts of a dissertation or project report

Part	Content
Cover sheet	Full title of project. Your name. Name of course of study of which this project is part.
Title page	Full title of project. Your name.
Acknowledgements	Who helped?
Introduction	Why did you do the work? What was the problem? If a literature survey is required, include a sub-heading as part of your introduction.
Methods	What materials and equipment did you use? How did you do the work?
Results	What are your findings?
Discussion	What do you make of your results? How do they compare with those of others?
Conclusions	What do you conclude? Can you answer any of the questions raised in your introduction?
Summary	What are your main findings?
References	List full bibliographic details (see page 134) of each source you have cited (in the introduction, methods and discussion sections).
Appendices	Include, for example, tables of data collected in your investigation and summarised in your *Results*.

A dissertation based on a literature search and reading, with supporting personal observations, will be written as an extended essay or review. As in any other essay, you will include an introduction and a conclusion but the body of the essay will comprise many more paragraphs than the compositions you have written previously. These paragraphs must be arranged in an effective order, and you will help yourself and your readers if you group closely related paragraphs below appropriate headings and sub-headings

In a project involving the collection and analysis of data, as well as the study of relevant published work, the project report may be arranged as in Table 11.1. Using the accepted headings, and knowing the kind of information readers expect to find below each heading, makes writing easier and helps readers to find the answers to their questions: What? Why? When? How? Where? Who?

Another type of project, preparing an instruction manual, may be appropriate in some courses (see *Prepare a set of instructions*, page 26). The project report could then be arranged as follows: cover; title page; acknowledgements; list of contents; description of equipment and naming of parts; operating instructions; maintenance instructions; servicing instructions; fault finding and fault correction. In such a technical report it is usual to number section headings (1, 2, 3, etc.) and to use decimal or point numbering for sub-headings (1.1, 1.2, 1.3, etc. in section 1) and, if necessary, for paragraphs under each sub-heading (1.1.1, 1.1.2, 1.1.3, etc.). The numbers help the writer to ensure that all sections and all paragraphs are in order, and they facilitate precise cross referencing (to sections, sub-sections and paragraphs instead of to pages).

In other courses a suitable project might be the preparation of a guide to the organisation and work of an agency, institution, firm or service. Such a report could be arranged as follows: cover; title page; acknowledgements; list of contents; introduction (including reason for existence of the agency, institution, etc., and your purpose in writing this report); method of inquiry (including how the information presented in your report was obtained, and what problems were encountered); results (of your inquiry); conclusions (including any recommendations); summary; sources of information; appendices (for example, tables of data from which the results reported were derived).

I hink about the headings that might be most suitable in your composition; and read the relevant parts of any syllabus, regulations or notes for guidance issued to the students taking your course. Then discuss your ideas with your supervisor. You need not necessarily be bound by conventions, but you must follow any instructions included in the regulations for your course or in the notes for guidance relating to your special study. The notes for guidance are intended to help you with your writing, to encourage uniformity in presentation, to make for easier reading by your assessors, and so to facilitate assessment.

Write from the start

Do not complete your investigations or your literature search and then start to write; and do not spend so much time on these things that you have no time to write (see Figure 9.1).

As soon as you and your supervisor have agreed on the title and scope of the work, try to allocate your time to thinking and planning, to the search for information or to collecting and analysing data, and to writing and revising your composition (see Figure 11.2). If your first draft is handwritten you will need to allow time for word processing (see page 183) and for preparing any illustrations (see page 88).

If you were writing an instruction manual you would try to ensure that it could be understood by anyone likely to be asked to perform the task in

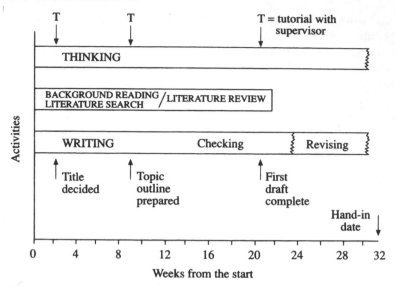

Figure 11.2 Preparing a dissertation: allocating your time to different tasks

question or to use the equipment described. Whatever you write, first try to identify your readers and then keep their needs in mind. Imagine, as you prepare your extended essay or project report, that you are writing not only for (a) your supervisor but also for (b) a second internal assessor who may know less than your supervisor about the subject of your composition, and for (c) an external examiner whose interests you do not know.

You are likely to be working on your special study at different times and in different places. You may record data when using laboratory equipment, or as part of field studies, or during interviews with different people. As part of a literature survey, you may make notes when working in different libraries, when using archive material to which you have limited access in a particular place, and when studying in your own room. As a result, unless you carry a laptop, much of the first draft of your composition, at least, will be handwritten.

When using a computer you must keep copies of your work in another place, on paper or on disk (see page 189), in case your computer is lost or stolen. Similarly, when working away from your computer, use a pad of wide-lined A4 paper and keep a carbon copy of everything you write. Then store the carbon copies, each evening, in appropriate files kept in your study. The use of a sheet of carbon paper is much easier, cheaper, and less time consuming, than the making of photocopies.

The more time you are spending on a composition, the more important it is that you keep an up-to-date copy in a safe place. Otherwise, if you lose your work and do not have a copy you will have to start all over again – from the beginning. At best this will interfere with your studies; at worst you may not have time to complete your composition.

Start writing as soon as you have decided what to study. Writing a first draft of the Introduction will concentrate your attention on the purpose of your composition and its relationship to other people's work. This should help you to see your limited objective, clearly stated in your terms of reference, in a wider perspective.

In a dissertation or extended essay, in any subject, the Introduction may include a *proposition*: a statement offered for consideration, which will be followed in the body of your composition by argument and by supporting evidence. Then in the last paragraph you may conclude that the proposition is probably a correct statement, or you may reject it, or you may state that you have insufficient evidence to reach either conclusion. Alternatively, your Introduction may include a *thesis*: a proposition you seek to maintain – again by argument and supporting evidence.

To *argue* in this context does not mean to disagree, but to present a case supported by evidence. You may present evidence for and then evidence against, or vice versa, depending on your conclusion. Or you may present the weak points in your argument first and the strongest last, leading to your conclusion. Or you may present the views of others first and your own last – as your conclusion. Whichever method you adopt, your argument will be the thread that runs through your whole composition, and the *evidence* presented may include recorded observations (data) and the results of your analysis of data (your results). Starting from a true premise (a proposition that is accepted as a fact until proved otherwise), a *logical argument* should lead to a valid conclusion. The word *valid* may refer to a reason, an objection or as here to a conclusion: it simply means that the reason, objection or conclusion is well founded.

In a project report, in science, the Introduction must include a statement of the *problem* investigated – which may be stated as a question. If an experiment is reported, the *hypothesis* tested – a possible answer to the question – should also be stated. A similar beginning may be appropriate in the report of any investigation in business or management: What is the problem? How might it be solved?

In a report of any investigation, write the Methods section as soon as you have decided how you will do the work. And then write an account of each part of your investigation, for the Results section, as soon as it is complete – so that, if necessary, you can easily check your work. Throughout the work, as they come to mind, make notes of any points you may wish to discuss. Then, when the work is complete, you can write the Discussion section of your report and revise all other sections.

As your work proceeds, prepare tables and illustrations to be included in any part of a dissertation or in the methods, results or discussion sections of a project report. There should be only one table or illustration on any page unless you wish to facilitate comparison. All tables and illustrations should be upright on the page so that readers do not need to turn the page to study them; and all drawings or diagrams that are to be compared must be drawn to the same scale (see page 91).

Search the literature

In a dissertation the whole work may be a critical literature review; and in a project report, in addition to citing relevant published work in the introduction, methods and discussion sections, a sub-section headed *Literature review* may be required as part of the introduction. Whether you are preparing an extended essay, a dissertation or a project report, finding relevant publications is a time-consuming but essential part of your work. Completing the literature review enables you:

1   to decide on the scope of your own composition;
2   to write about your own findings in the context of previous work, including recent work;
3   to recognise inconsistencies, different interpretations of evidence, differences of opinion, and gaps in your knowledge or understanding;
4   to comment upon and discuss the work of others, and establish the originality of your own work; and, perhaps,
5   to add to what is known.

In undertaking a literature review, start with your supervisor's suggestions and any references provided. Make use of publications available in your own library and in other convenient libraries (see pages 115 to 125).

In some subjects most of the information you require may be available in books, including introductory textbooks, advanced treatises, and research monographs. In other subjects you may find little useful information in books. One reason for this is that publishers may find it uneconomic to produce up-to-date books for specialists – because few people are likely to buy them, and because an author may have to complete a literature survey a year or more before a book's publication date.

The more specialised your work, or the more recent the published work you need to read, the less you will be able to rely on books and the more you will need to look at journals that publish the original work of specialists (see page 121). For the most recent published papers, because your own library can subscribe to only a few of the thousands of journals published each year, you will need to use relevant abstracting and indexing services (for example, see Table 9.3). However, you should be aware of relevant review publications in your subject. Some of these are journals, but publish only review articles – each article being a review of the literature on a specialised aspect of a subject. Others are books, in which each chapter is a review article.

Useful information on topics of current interest may also be included in conference proceedings (in which each chapter is a paper read at a conference), and in official reports published, for example, by international organisations and government departments (each of which will conclude with recommendations).

In addition to leaflets on how to use their catalogues, most academic libraries provide concise guides to the literature on different subjects, and you should ask for the guide to each of the subjects in which you are interested.

To find books relevant to your dissertation or project, use the catalogues of your own library and those of other convenient libraries (see page 119). And to find whether or not a book in which you are interested is in print consult an on-line bibliographic database (see page 124). For older books, consult databases that include the catalogues of major libraries (see Table 9.3).

To find reports of the most recent work, you may scan the contents pages of selected journals in your library, or see the titles of papers, the contents pages of journals, and abstracts of papers, on screen, by entering key words at a computer terminal connected to electronic databases (see Table 9.3). These key words (search terms) must be selected carefully (see page 122) so that they help you find only relevant publications.

Keep a note of the search terms you use, of the issues of journals you have searched, and of their location. Then if some journals are unavailable you can come back to them later to continue your search when more issues of these journals have been published. Start with the most recent issue of each journal. If you find a paper that interests you it will refer to earlier papers that are also likely to be of interest, some of which may be review articles.

Advantages of using computer-based information retrieval include the following.

1   You can search many years' issues of an abstracting journal in a few minutes.
2   You can access more sources of information, including some databases available only on-line, than would otherwise be possible.

3   You can search for any key word in title, abstract and description fields.

4   You can obtain a printout of complete bibliographic details as the search is performed; and you can order copies of references selected from this list.

5   The search can be interactive: you can change the search terms (key words) in response to information obtained.

6   You can arrange for a satisfactory search to be repeated using the same key words each time a database is updated, and you can ask to be sent bibliographic details of any new references located.

Disadvantages of online searching include the following.

1   Indexing of database records may be inconsistent.

2   Databases may include details of journals published in recent years only.

3   The databases covered may be biased towards the publications of one country.

Although an online search will include more publications than a manual search, and details of many relevant references are likely to be obtained, additional useful sources of information will be found if you also do a manual search. If you have time, therefore, it is best to do both: a manual search for the library resources available to you locally, and an online search for resources that would otherwise be inaccessible.

However you work, in a thorough search you are likely to find references to many more publications than you have time to read. So try to reduce your list to manageable proportions. For some you may decide from the title that they are unlikely to be useful. For each of the others you must decide – from the author's name, the title of the publication, a published abstract, or a reference in a review article – that it is (a) likely to be of immediate interest, or (b) unlikely to be a key work, or (c) unlikely to be relevant to your present needs. You may then be in a position to decide, perhaps after further discussion with your supervisor, whether or not you should try to obtain on inter-library loan any of the publications that are not available locally.

Inter-library loans are expensive, so a library may impose restrictions as to how many, if any, you are allowed free of charge. So you will probably send for only those few you feel are essential for the satisfactory completion of your work. You will probably have to rely mainly on the resources of local libraries, those of libraries you are able to visit when on vacation, and materials available via the internet or via an intranet.

Start by selecting a few publications that you think should be useful. Record complete bibliographic details (see pages 128–9) of each publication you intend to consult, either on an A6 index card (148 × 105 mm) or at the top of a sheet of wide-lined A4 paper. Before making further notes, also record both the name of the library from which you obtained the publication and the publication's book or shelf number so that you can find it again easily if you need to. If you request a publication on inter-library loan, record the date of your request.

When you have any publication in your hands, first check that your record of its bibliographic details is complete and correct, because there may be mistakes in the indexes, abstracts and other publications from which you copied this information. Then evaluate the publication by reading the abstract, the introduction and the conclusions, and by studying any tables and figures. If it is of interest, scan the section headings, and decide: (a) how much of it you must study – one page, one part or the whole work; or (b) that it is not essential reading but may be of interest later – after you have completed more urgent tasks.

If you use loose-leaf A4 paper for your notes, you can file any photocopies with your notes – in the most appropriate place. But do not allow making a photocopy to become an alternative to reading an important publication critically, as soon as is convenient after you receive it, and making your own notes.

For a student preparing a dissertation or project report there is probably no advantage in entering references on a computer database, unless there is some exceptional reason for doing so. It is easy to cope with the limited number of references likely to be involved, by keeping your records in alphabetical order by author on A6 index cards or, as recommended on page 158, on A4 paper. Both have the advantage of being portable – enabling you to enter bibliographic details as you undertake a search, to make notes on the same card or sheet, and to interleave further notes or photocopies at any time, wherever you are working.

Review the literature

You must cite sources in support of any reference you make to published evidence, but if you read critically throughout your course you will find many instances in which experts disagree about the interpretation of evidence, especially if there is conflicting evidence. This is why students may be encouraged to develop a healthy scepticism and to be prepared to question everything. Do not accept published statements or conclusions as being correct just because the author is an acknowledged authority. Always consider the evidence presented in relation to other evidence and your own experience. Read critically, and with an enquiring mind. Is this relevant? Is it true? What is the evidence? What are the implications? The results of such critical thinking will be apparent in your writing.

You will recognise *assertions* (things stated as if they were true, but for which evidence is not provided by the writer), *assumptions* (things assumed to be true by the writer, but which may not be), *facts* (things that on the basis of all the evidence at present available are generally accepted as true statements), and *speculation* (which may or may not be well founded, and so could be helpful or misleading). You will draw attention to conflicting statements, to *issues* (points of disagreement) and to *opinions* (views based on insufficient evidence, personal experience or preconceived ideas, but which are not necessarily correct). And you may make comparisons, recognise connections, suggest original interpretations, and come to your own conclusions, or point out the need for further research.

There may be times, as you read and accumulate your notes, when you feel bogged down in the conflicting interpretations of evidence, and find it impossible to refer to all the available sources of information or cope with the wealth of detail (see Figure 9.1). Do not be discouraged by this; but do be selective in your search for information. In your reading you will come across many side-issues that you find interesting and may like to return to when you have time. But do not digress: keep your title and your terms of reference in mind and concentrate on material relevant to your immediate needs.

Be prepared to change your mind as you learn more and achieve a deeper understanding. Part of the pleasure to be gained from reading and writing comes not only from your increasing knowledge and understanding of the subject itself but also from the enlightenment that comes from enlarging your view of the world. And part comes from the satisfaction gained from shaping and presenting your thoughts for your own later consideration – and so as to influence the thoughts and actions of others.

Improve your writing

Work on your first draft

To make your work easier, write on one side only of each sheet of paper. Write each heading, each sub-heading, and even each paragraph on a separate sheet; and prepare each table and illustration on a separate sheet. This will help you: (a) to ensure that each paragraph deals with only one topic, (b) to keep information on each topic in one place, (c) to avoid unintentional repetition, (d) to incorporate additional material in the most appropriate place, change the order of presentation and remove unwanted material easily, and (e) to rewrite paragraphs when necessary without having to rewrite the whole of your composition. In this way, as when word processing, while you are working your handwritten draft will always be an up-to-date progress report.

If you have kept notes, as suggested on page 128, you will have recorded complete bibliographic details of each source cited in your composition – at the top of a separate page of your notes (or on an index card). When your work is otherwise complete, these can be removed from your file and the details listed in alphabetical order after the heading *Bibliography* or *References*, as appropriate (see page 134). Remember to list only publications you have studied as part of your work. Your assessors should be impressed: (a) by the thoroughness of your search and your ability to select and evaluate relevant sources, not by the length of your list of sources, and (b) if you have an oral examination by your ability to speak knowledgeably about the publications listed.

You will probably have revised or rewritten your Introduction several times, and you must check it again when your composition is otherwise complete. Try to ensure that the reader is interested and favourably impressed at the start. However, bear in mind that readers may read your summary or abstract first – even though this is the last thing you write – so it too requires much thought.

A summary, if one is required, will come at the end of your composition (see Table 11.1, page 156); so the reader will also be able to refer to the other sections. But you may be required to provide an abstract, instead of a summary, and this may be placed immediately after the title. If an extra copy of the abstract is required, this will probably be sent to an external examiner – who may see it first without the rest of your composition. The difference between an abstract and a summary, therefore, is that an abstract may have to stand alone – representing your work in the absence of the composition as a whole, just as when you read abstracts in an abstracting journal or bibliographic database.

Check your composition

You cannot check a long composition properly by reading it through once or twice. You must check one thing at a time.

1   Are the cover and title pages complete? Do they provide all the information required by your assessors? For example, see Table 11.1.

2   Does the title provide the best concise description of the contents of your composition?

3   Do you need a contents page? If you do, make sure all the headings and sub-headings are included, are in order, and are identical with those used in your composition.

4   Does each part of your composition start with a main heading at the top of a page?

5   Are the purpose and scope of your composition (or your terms of reference) stated clearly and concisely in the Introduction? Is everything included in your composition relevant to the title? Do you keep within the scope of the work as stated in your Introduction; and comply with your terms of reference?

6   Has anything essential been omitted? Are all your readers' questions answered (see page 156)? Are your conclusions clearly stated?

7   Is each paragraph necessary? Is it in the best place? Is the connection between paragraphs clear? Does the end of each paragraph lead smoothly into the next?

8   Is the composition well balanced? Is each of your main points clearly and forcefully expressed? Is anything original emphasised sufficiently?

9   Is each statement accurate, based on sufficient evidence, free from contradictions, and free from errors of omission?

10 Are there any words, such as few or many, that should be replaced by numbers?

11 Are there any mistakes in spelling or grammar?

12 Could the meaning of any sentence be better expressed? Is each sentence easy to read? Does it sound well when read aloud? Does each sentence lead the reader smoothly into the next?

13 Are any technical terms, symbols or abbreviations sufficiently explained, and used consistently and correctly?

14 Are all your sources cited correctly? If your notes for guidance do not give clear instructions on the method to be used (see pages 132–3), ask your supervisor for advice.

15 Are all sources cited in your composition listed correctly and in the right order at the end, after the heading Bibliography or References, as appropriate (see page 165)?

16 Are all figures, tables and pages numbered and in order?

17 Have you referred to each figure and each table at least once in the text? Is any information presented in a table and repeated in a diagram? Do the tables and diagrams support the text, without unnecessary repetition?

18 Does the composition look neat?

19 Have you obeyed all the instructions in your course guide, or provided as separate notes for guidance on your special study? See also page 157.

When you have written, checked and corrected your first draft, your supervisor may like to read it and may suggest improvements. Then ask someone else to read your work. Readers may find inconsistencies or mistakes, sentences and paragraphs that are irrelevant or out of place, and parts that are ambiguous or difficult to understand. Consider their comments or suggestions carefully; then make any necessary additions, deletions or corrections before handing in your composition for assessment.

12 Writing letters and applications

Your success as a student will depend largely on your ability to express your thoughts clearly in writing. And in any career based on your studies your value to your employer will depend not only on your knowledge and experience but also on your ability to communicate your thoughts effectively in clear instructions, concise reports, and business correspondence. However, long before this, when applying for admission to a course of study or for employment, writing a good letter will increase your chances of being selected for interview. Such a composition, although short, could turn out to be the most important you ever write.

Writing a good letter

Letter writing may seem far removed from answering questions in coursework and examinations, but these very different kinds of communications should have many common characteristics (see Table 3.1).

If you can write a good letter, to obtain just the information you need or to provide just the information someone else needs, then you probably appreciate that the first consideration in letter writing – as in any other communication – is what the reader needs to know. When initiating any correspondence, consider what you would like to know, how to make your requirements clear, and how your words are likely to affect the reader. Before replying to any communication, consider what information must be included, why it is required, and by whom.

When you write to people you know, their opinion of you is not entirely based on what and how you write. But when you write business letters to people whom you have never met they will judge you in the only way they can: by your writing. You should therefore take particular care over the content, layout and appearance of every business letter to ensure that it makes a favourable impression on the recipient (see Table 1.1).

The organisation of all except the shortest letter can be improved, and its length reduced, if you make a few notes of points you must emphasise

Table 12.1 Different kinds of letters and their tone

Purpose of letter	Tone
Request for details (for example, of a course of study, an appointment or an item of equipment)	Clear, simple, direct and courteous
Invitation to a speaker	
Application for employment	Clear, direct and factual. Confident but not aggressive
Complaint	Clear and direct but not aggressive
Reply (to an enquiry, or complaint) giving information, instruction or explanation. Answering all questions raised in the enquiry	Clear, direct, informative, polite, helpful, and sincere
Acknowledgement (for example, of an application, complaint, enquiry)	Simple and direct
Acknowledgement by postcard	Discreet
Letter of thanks	Appreciative

and then number them in an effective order. Then, having decided what to say, convey your message simply, clearly, concisely, and courteously. These are the essentials.

Try to put yourself in the place of the recipient as you read each letter before signing it. A good letter is one that creates a favourable impression on the recipient and enables you to convey information pleasurably, or to obtain the action or information you require.

When you write a business letter, remember there is no special *business English*. The only rule is to avoid words and phrases that you would not use in other kinds of writing (for example, 'Please find enclosed', 'I remain your obedient servant', and similar outmoded expressions), and to omit superfluous introductory phrases (for example, 'I am writing to let you know that . . .').

Most letters are written on one side of one sheet of paper, so writing letters can provide frequent opportunities to improve your writing without occupying too much of your time.

In a few words you must pass on your message and create the right atmosphere between yourself and the person addressed. The tone of each letter will depend on your purpose (see Table 12.1) but no letter should be discourteous.

A formal letter is addressed to a business or organisation (see Tables 12.2 and 12.3) and a less formal letter to an individual by name (see Table 12.4).

Table 12.2 Layout of a formal business letter

Address
of sender[a]

Position
and address
of recipient[b]

Date[c]

Salutation[d]

Subject heading[e]

1 State your business.

2 Provide necessary supporting details.

3 State your conclusion or indicate the action required.

Complimentary close[d]

Signature[f]

Name and position of sender

Enclosures (a list)

An alphanumeric reference
(for example, initials of person signing letter and a number)

Notes
a Words such as company (Co.) may be abbreviated. Otherwise, addresses should not be punctuated.
b The position and address of the recipient must be as on the envelope.
c The date (on which letter is signed and posted) should be written in full (see page 86), without punctuation.
d The salutation should be Dear Sir, Dear Sirs, or Dear Madam, and the complimentary close either Yours faithfully or Yours truly, depending on national custom.
e The heading should be in italics or underlined.
f Your signature should be legible.

Table 12.3 Example of a formal business letter

Your
address[a]

The Academic Registrar[b]
Name of institution
and full postal address

Date[c]

Dear Sir/Madam[d]

Subject in which you are interested

Please send details of your course in ....

I shall be taking my ....examinations
in two years' time , In the following subjects: ....
and ....

I should be grateful if you would also confirm that these subjects do provide
a satisfactory basis for your course or let me know of any special admission
requirements.

Yours faithfully[e]

Signature[f]

Alphanumeric reference
(is not essential in a private business letter)

Notes
a Addresses should not be punctuated.
b The position, not the name of the recipient, and address, as on the envelope.
c The date (on which letter is signed and posted) should be written in full (see page 86),
   without punctuation.
d The salutation should be Dear Sir, or Dear Madam, or Dear Sir/Madam.
e The complimentary close should be either Yours faithfully or Yours truly, depending on
   national custom.
f Your signature should be legible.

Table 12.4 Layout of a less formal business letter

	Address of sender[a]
Name[b] and address of recipient	
	Date[c]
Salutation[d]	
Subject heading	
State your business.	
Provide necessary supporting details.	
State your conclusion or your requirements.	
Complimentary close[e]	
Signature[f]	
Name and position of sender	
Enclosures (a list)	
Alphanumeric reference (for example, initials of person signing letter and a number)	

Notes
a Words such as company (Co.) may be abbreviated. Otherwise, addresses should not be punctuated.
b The name, position and address of the recipient must be as on the envelope.
c The date (on which letter is signed and posted) should be written in full (see page 86), without punctuation.
d The salutation should include the name and title of the recipient.
e The complimentary close is normally Yours sincerely.
f Your signature should be legible.

Table 12.5 How to use a postcard

A Correct use

                                                    Date signed and posted

Omit salutation. Just write your message.

Note that a postcard is likely to be read by other people before it is seen by the person addressed. So when you use a postcard to acknowledge the receipt of a letter do not make public the contents or purpose of the letter. It is enough to say 'Receipt of your communication dated .... ref. .... is acknowledged'.

Omit complimentary close

Your signature

Your name and
postal address

B An example

                                                    Date signed and posted

Thank your for your letter of ....

Your reference: ....
which is receiving attention.

Your signature

Your position and
address

Alphanumeric reference, as in a business letter

A less formal letter may be used in business when addressing a particular person, especially if the correspondents have met or know each other well from conversations on the telephone or from previous correspondence (see Table 12.4).

To keep each communication short and to the point, any necessary supporting details or further information should be referred to briefly in the letter but sent as an enclosure. Each enclosure should begin with a concise title; and all enclosures should be listed by their titles at the end of the letter (below the heading *Enclosures*).

The initiator of any correspondence should precede the message by a precise and specific subject heading that makes clear what the message is to be about (and should not therefore begin with the abbreviation *re.*, meaning about). However, the heading is not part of the message. So always make your purpose clear in the first sentence. For example, begin: 'Please send . . .', or 'I should be grateful if you would . . .'.

The reply, and any further correspondence, should have an identical subject heading and should begin 'Thank you for your letter of . . . about . . .'. From these beginnings both the writer and the recipient know immediately what each communication is about (see Tables 12.2 to 12.5 on pages 170–3).

Answer every letter promptly. A prompt reply makes for efficiency, enabling you to complete a task, and your efficiency will impress the recipient favourably. Before replying to a letter, read it carefully. Then make sure you answer all the writer's questions. If there is some good reason for delaying your reply, acknowledge receipt of the letter by postcard (see Table 12.5B), and then send your reply as soon as you can.

Because it may be read by other people, before it is seen by the addressee, never write anything confidential on a postcard. It is usually sufficient to write: 'Thank you for your communication dated . . . which is receiving attention.'

Keep a copy of every written communication you send and of any reply; and keep every important document received with the reply. Copies of your correspondence are essential for your own reference, and so that anyone else with access to your files can, if necessary, act for you in your absence.

Telephone conversations have not replaced written communications, sent by post or e-mail, as the most effective method of conducting business (see Figure 12.1). One reason for this is that misunderstandings are possible unless both parties have an accurate record of any important conversation: and all business conversations are important. So, anything agreed on the telephone must be confirmed in writing, normally on the same day as the telephone call.

It could be easier and quicker to write a letter

Figure 12.1 In business a letter or e-mail is usually a more satisfactory means of communication than a telephone conversation

Because every letter and every e-mail must fit into the files of both the sender and the recipient, it should deal with one subject only. If you have to write to anyone about more than one subject, deal with these subjects in separate communications (even if these are to be sent by post in one envelope).

Forms of address, to be used on envelopes, are suggested in Table 12.6. Ensure that the address on the envelope is identical with that used in your letter, because you may need to check, later, from your copy of the letter, that the envelope was correctly addressed. If appropriate, you may wish to write *Confidential* in the top left-hand corner of the envelope.

Write your own address on the back of the envelope, in the top left-hand corner, in small writing, so that if for any reason it cannot be delivered it can be returned to you.

Table 12.6 Forms of address (to be used on envelopes)

Mr John Smith (if John Smith is an adult)
Mrs John Smith (when addressed as John Smith's wife)[a]
John Smith Esquire (if you wish to indicate your respect)[b]
Miss Jean Smith (if Jean Smith is unmarried)[c]
Master John Smith (if John Smith is a child)
John Smith (if John Smith is an adolescent)
Miss Jean Smith BA PhD or Dr Jean Smith[c]
Messrs John Smith & Sons[d]

Notes
a A married woman, especially if in business or a profession, may prefer to use her maiden name.
b This form of address is now rarely used, but if it is written after the surname no other title should be written before the surname.
c In business correspondence a woman should indicate, below her signature, how she wishes to be addressed: for example as Miss Jean Smith, Ms Jean Smith or Mrs John Smith.
d The prefix Messrs (French Messieurs) as the plural of Mr is acceptable when addressing firms with personal names (for example, Messrs John Smith & Sons). It is not used when addressing limited companies or firms that do not trade under a surname. Most business letters are addressed to The Secretary or to The Manager, for example, or to an individual by name.

For guidance on the correct use of titles and other distinguishing marks of honour or office, see *Titles and Forms of Address*, London, A. and C. Black.

Communicating by electronic mail

Even if your computer contains up-to-date virus-detecting software, do not open an attachment to any incoming e-mail from an unknown source. It could be contaminated with computer viruses (see *Looking after your documents*, page 189).

The layout of an e-mail message is not determined by the sender but by the computer software used. A standard template, similar to a memorandum form, is provided on the screen. The postal address is replaced by an e-mail address. As in a memorandum, the names of both the recipient and the sender precede the message, which starts with a subject heading, and there is neither a salutation nor a complimentary close.

All that is necessary in replying to a communication is to insert your message, ensuring that you include: (a) an alphanumeric reference as part of the subject heading, for purposes of filing – and, if necessary, (b) the name of your organisation and your job title.

Communication by e-mail is easy, but it should not be casual or ill considered. Each message should be in grammatically correct English, with correct spelling and punctuation. However short, like every other communication it should be prepared in four stages. Always: think, plan, write, and then check your work – and revise it if necessary (see page 50).

Unless encrypted by a secure server, e-mail messages can be intercepted. So never send confidential information by e-mail; and never forward (circulate) a message without considering who is entitled to receive the information it contains. Also, never write anything that might embarrass others or cause offence, and bear in mind: (a) that many employers use security products in an attempt to prevent fraud and other misuses of e-mail; and (b) that e-mail messages may be stored for years in an organisation's backup files. Messages sent by e-mail are neither as private nor as ephemeral as some people may think.

Correspondence should normally be dealt with promptly (see page 174) but because with e-mail it is possible to reply immediately, upon receipt of a message, the temptation to do so may have to be resisted – for several reasons. First, incoming e-mail messages should be placed in order of priority, with other correspondence and other tasks, on your job list (see page 10). Second, even if you acknowledge receipt of an e-mail message immediately, time should be allocated to any necessary thought, consultation or research before you write a considered reply. Special care is needed to ensure that confidential information is not disclosed inadvertently as a result of replying in haste. Third, and in particular, if any message irritates or annoys you it is essential that you give yourself the time for reflection that you would have had if an immediate response had not been possible.

The best response to any communication that annoys you, if a reply is needed, is to reply only to the points that must be answered (without giving any indication of your annoyance). This is true whether or not you are using e-mail. Words written in anger, which you may later regret and which others will not forget, should not be allowed to find their way into someone else's records. Remember also that the laws of libel apply to e-mail as to any other written communication.

Take as much care in deciding to whom you should send each e-mail message as you would take in deciding who should receive copies of a letter or memorandum. Like any other communication, an e-mail message should be sent only to the person or persons who require the information it contains, not thoughtlessly to others who do not need to be informed.

In responding to an e-mail message it is possible to 'Send', or to 'Send (with history)'. However, sending with history results in many people receiving copies of large numbers of earlier communications, which they do not need and which they should not have been sent. So, usually prefer 'Send'.

Another feature of e-mail, contributing to information overload, is that it is easier to append unprocessed blocks of text from other documents, or (worse) whole documents, than to trouble to extract and summarise relevant parts before sending just the information the receiver needs.

Improve your writing

Applying for employment

Writing a letter is a test of one's ability to communicate effectively – using appropriate language. It can be set as an exercise that most students will find useful and interesting. So this is a good way to start teaching, or learning, the essentials of clear, concise and courteous writing.

Write a letter applying for a vacation job or for the kind of work you would like as a career. Remember that the content of your letter and the way the information is presented are usually the only evidence available to an employer as to whether or not an applicant could be useful as an employee. As with any business letter, take care over the appearance of your application.

> Use unlined white paper (size A4 = 210×297 mm).
> Write legibly or use a word processor.
> Leave adequate margins.
> Keep a copy.
> Fold the paper once or twice so that it fits neatly into the envelope.
> Write your own address on the back of the envelope, in the top left-hand corner, in small writing, so that if for any reason it cannot be delivered it can be returned to you.

The success of your application, in enabling you to obtain an interview, will depend not only on the care with which you prepare the application but also on your interests and suitability as indicated in your application.

An application for employment is usually in two parts: a letter of application (see Table 12.7) and a curriculum vitae (c.v.) or résumé (see Table 12.8 on page 180).

In the letter you ask to be considered for this particular vacancy and state why you are applying: for example, why you consider that you are suitable and why you think that you would find the work interesting.

Table 12.7 Example of a letter of application

The Personnel Manager	Your
Name of organisation	address
and address	
(as in advertisement)	

Date signed and posted

Dear Sir (or Dear Madam)

Post for which you are applying

Please consider this application for the post of ....

(ref. .... advertised in ....

on ....

I shall be completing an honours degree course in ....

at .... on ....

At school I was .... and at university I have

taken an active part in ....

In vacations I have worked ....

and I have travelled in ....

I enjoy working with other people and should like to make a career

in .... I have a particular interest

in .... My curriculum vitae is enclosed.

I shall be taking my final examinations in .... Otherwise,

I am available for interview at any time.

Yours faithfully

Enc. Curriculum vitae

In the curriculum vitae, state your name, date of birth, nationality, postal address and telephone number. Name your school. List the subjects you studied or are studying at school, and give the results of any examinations.

Start each entry with the dates attended or the dates examinations were taken. Similarly, name your college or university, list the subjects you are studying and give the results of any examinations.

List your non-academic interests. Mention any weekend or vacation work, or other experience, and emphasise anything relevant to the work for which you are now applying.

Table 12.8 Example of a curriculum vitae or résumé

Curriculum vitae

Thomas Jones   Date of birth ....
British
Single
Home adress
Telephone number

Dates attended and name of school
Dates examinations taken and grades obtained
with subjects listed in the order most appropriate for this application

Dates attended and name of college and/or university
Courses taken

Dates of examinations and grades obtained

Date of final examinations
Non-academic interests and details of any vacation work

Names and postal addresses of two referees: one with knowledge of your
non-academic interests and the other able to speak of your recent work as
a student or in other employment.

End with a legible signature and the date.

Give the names of two or three referees: preferably one who can speak of
your character and non-academic interests; and at least one who can speak
about your recent work (as a student or in other employment). Choose
your referees carefully for each application, to make sure they are appropriate. Remember to ask their permission before you give their names; and it
may help them to support your applications if you keep them informed
about the kinds of work for which you are applying and why you think you
would find it interesting.

Your curriculum vitae, with dates first in each entry, is a summary of all the important events and achievements in your life that are likely to interest *this employer*. If possible, fit this information on one side of one sheet of paper. Every year since you left school must be accounted for: otherwise the reader is likely to suspect that you have something to hide.

As in any other composition, consider your readers. If the post has been advertised study the requirements emphasised in the advertisement. Then write for further details and an application form. The further details will tell you more about the post advertised and about the employer.

If there is an application form, use it instead of your curriculum vitae. Before writing anything on the application form, read it carefully and prepare a draft of your answers to the questions on a separate sheet of paper. This will enable you: (a) to keep the form clean and unfolded until you are ready to use it; (b) to ensure that you are able to provide the information required in the spaces available; (c) to write and revise each entry until you are satisfied that it is the best answer you can give to the question asked; (d) to check your answers to make sure you have obeyed any instructions (for example to write in block letters or to use black ink); and (e) to copy your answers neatly on to a photocopy of the form. Note that you must answer all questions even if in answering some questions you write only *none* or *not applicable*.

It is best to make corrections and improvements on a first draft of your application until you are satisfied that you know how best to present yourself in each application. Then, if there is time, put your draft on one side at least overnight. When you read it again, try to think how the recipient will react. Imagine that the reader will be middle-aged, and that he or she will be looking for someone with respect for authority, with a positive personality, who is likely to get along well with other people and accept responsibility. You may also find it helpful to ask someone whose judgement you respect to read and comment on your draft.

If your covering letter and the entries on an application form are handwritten, ensure that the writing is legible and neat. Any supporting papers sent as enclosures should, if practicable, be word processed – as, if there is no application form, should your curriculum vitae. Post your application to arrive before the closing date.

Making the most of yourself in an application is clearly time-consuming, but it is worth spending several hours on this task if you are trying to obtain suitable employment for a whole vacation or possibly for the rest of your working life.

13 Your computer as an aid to writing

Using your computer

Improving your keyboard skills

Many computer users hand-write at least the first draft of anything other than a very short composition so that they can work fast enough to allow their thoughts and their written words to flow. Then they spend more time than should be necessary word processing later drafts. That is to say, they are handicapped when using a computer by their poor keyboard skills.

Unless you can touch type, when using a computer for word processing, (a) you will not be able to look at handwritten notes, drafts or data sheets, from which you are copying, as you key in words and numbers; (b) you will not be able to work as fast as if you knew how to use the keyboard properly; and (c) you will find it difficult to break bad habits if you decide later to learn touch typing.

So if you cannot touch type you are advised to learn, *preferably before using a computer for word processing*. Then you know from the start which letter keys and which number keys to strike with each finger and can strike them without looking at your computer keyboard. You could learn from a book that includes basic instructions and graded exercises, or attend a class on keyboard skills, or buy a computer program that provides on-screen instruction. Then, if you use a computer regularly, with frequent practice you should soon be touch typing on your computer keyboard faster than you can write with a pen.

Word processing

Your computer has a memory but no intelligence. It is a tool that can make writing easier, but you still have to do the thinking at each stage in composition. You must think and plan before writing, and take care when writing, even though it is easy to make changes after writing.

When working on a screen, as in writing with a pen, you must: (a) make notes as you think about what is required; (b) re-arrange your notes below appropriate headings as you prepare the topic outline for your composition; (c) choose and arrange words carefully as you write to ensure you express your thoughts clearly and simply; and then (d) check, correct and if necessary revise your work (see pages 165–7).

Whether a composition is handwritten or word-processed, nothing can be done after writing – by checking and revising – to compensate for devoting insufficient time to thinking and to planning before starting to write. But if you give enough thought to the needs of the reader before you write (to content and presentation, see page 158) there should not be much wrong with your first draft of any composition.

If, because you are word processing, you (a) prepare a topic outline on the screen, (b) add to it from time to time (as new thoughts come to mind), and (c) reconsider the wording as you move things around (to make sense of the revised order of your sentences and paragraphs), or (d) correct mistakes or typing errors (as they capture your attention), you will be thinking and planning as you write. You will not be able to work as fast as if you were to think first and then use your topic outline as a guide when writing.

You may be required to word-process some of your compositions in coursework, but if you were to word process them all you would find it very difficult to do your best work in examinations. Then: (a) you have to think, plan and write quickly; (b) you have very little time in which to check each composition; (c) you have to get things right first time; and (d) even if you are allowed to use a computer you are unlikely to have time to move things around using cut and paste, to revise the pasted material so that it makes sense in its new position, or to use a spell checker. In short, in most examinations students have to use handwriting if they are to do the best work of which they are capable in the limited time available.

In coursework you can spend more time on thinking and planning than you could spare in an examination. Nevertheless, you are advised not to get so much into the habit of writing at a computer keyboard that you are unable to produce a satisfactory handwritten first draft of a composition in about the time that would be available for you to prepare a good answer to a similar question in an examination – when you would not be able to use a word processor.

Furthermore, in coursework, students who can prepare a neat handwritten first draft that is legible and well presented – so that it does not need to be revised – should not be required (as they are on many courses) to waste their time word processing a second draft just to change their handwriting into print.

Both students and their assessors should accept that a composition can be well presented without its being word-processed (see page 43). As a student you must develop the ability to write quickly and to get things right the first time in tests and examinations; and for practice in coursework you are advised to hand-write at least the first draft of each composition quickly in about the time that would be available in an examination (see page 149).

Preparing a word-processed document

When word processing you format a document before starting to write (setting margins and choosing line spacing, print size, typeface, etc.). Then you can produce pages of text, including tables and illustrations, with a print quality similar to that of a book. However, as you are not writing a book, your work will be easier to read if you do not justify right-hand margins.

When working on a project report you may be given notes for guidance that state clearly how your composition is to be laid out. Such notes help to ensure that all students taking the same subject present their work in a similar way; and this facilitates assessment. Any instructions provided by your assessor, or the regulations of your examining body, must obviously take precedence over any advice included here.

The following instructions will help you to ensure that a word-processed document is well presented, whether it is word processed for you or you do the work yourself.

1 Use A4 paper.
2 Leave a 40 mm margin on the left, and margins of about 25 mm on the right, top and bottom of each page.
3 Use a standard typeface (not italic) and type in double spacing on one side of each sheet only. A 12 point **Times New Roman** (a *serif* type-face) is suitable for most purposes; but a *sans serif* typeface (for example, **Arial**) may be preferred for the letters and numbers on drawings and diagrams.
4 Start with the title, your name and the date, as with a handwritten composition (see page 50). In a long composition (for example, a project report) include separate cover and title pages, and a list of contents; then start each section with a main heading at the top of a new sheet. Centre main headings, but not sub-headings.
5 Use capitals, bold print and italics for different grades of headings (see page 34), and give most headings a line to themselves – for emphasis. Do not underline them; and do not use bold, italics or underlining to emphasise words (as is done in some textbooks). Use italic print in the text only for words that should be underlined in handwriting (see page 104).
6 When writing in capital letters (for example, for main headings) leave

two spaces between words. Leave one space after a comma, semicolon, colon or full stop; and one space after a contraction (for example Dr T. D. Jones) but leave no spaces between the letters of an acronym (for example, UNESCO). Always leave a space between an arabic numeral and an SI unit of measurement (for example 1 m = one metre: see page 87).

7 Leave twice as much space between paragraphs as between the lines within paragraphs; and be consistent in the amount of space you leave before and after sub-headings (as in a book).

8 Prepare each table on a separate sheet, with any essential footnotes below the table (see page 90) but with no other words on the same sheet. Refer to each table at least once in the text; and in the completed composition either place each table near to where it is mentioned first in the text or place all your tables together in an appendix.

9 When all your tables and figures have been inserted, number all the pages (except the cover, title and contents pages) with arabic numerals at the top right-hand corner.

10 Then add page numbers next to the headings on the contents pages.

11 Keep a copy.

Checking a word-processed document

Because with a word processor it is so easy to make additions and deletions, to cut and paste, and to copy, great care is needed when checking or revising any document to ensure that it reads well, with no words missing and no words, sentences or paragraphs duplicated or out of place (see *Check your answer*, page 41, and *Check your composition*, page 166).

Great care is also needed to ensure that material down loaded from the internet, or cut from other electronic sources, is not inadvertently pasted without appropriate acknowledgement into a document you are preparing (see originality, page 23; plagiarism, page 24; and citing sources, page 132).

Checking spelling Use the spell checker on your computer. It will help you to correct typing errors and spelling mistakes, and so to improve your spelling. However, although a spell checker ensures that each word used is spelt correctly (in American English or British English according to your requirements) it does not ensure that it is the right word (see page 54). For example, does the spelling and grammar checker on your computer draw attention to any errors when you type the following sentences?

I advice you to consider the following advise.

There's too mistakes in the last sentence.

There are, in fact, two mistakes in each of these sentences. They should read:

> I advise you to consider the following advice.
>
> There're two mistakes . . . (There's means there is).

However, in scholarly writing it is best to avoid colloquial language by writing:

> There are two mistakes . . .

Also, do not allow a spell checker to spell-check and change, automatically, specialist terms, abbreviations, acronyms or proper names (of people and places) unless these are correct in your computer's spell-check dictionary. It would be embarrassing, for example, if the computer changed Mr Charlton's surname to Charlotte or, worse, to Charlatan – and you did not notice the mistake when checking the document.

Checking grammar If you use grammar-checking software it may help you to ensure that a sentence is grammatically correct (according to the rules used in writing the program) but it will not ensure that the sentence makes sense or that its meaning is as you intended. That is to say, the changes suggested by a grammar checker may not be improvements.

The rules applied by copy-editors when correcting spelling and grammar differ in different countries, as do those applied by people writing computer software, because of differences of opinion as to what is acceptable to different English-speaking peoples. There is also the problem that some things considered to be rules by some experts are considered by others to be no more than matters of opinion. Also, the language changes: some rules once applied strictly by some publishers are now less rigidly applied, or are not applied, even by these same publishers.

It is necessary to take an interest in words (in vocabulary) and in the arrangement of words (syntax) so that you can formulate and express your own thoughts. Then, in speaking and in writing, for most purposes a good sentence is one in which: (a) you express your meaning as clearly and simply as you can, and (b) a listener takes your meaning correctly on hearing, and a reader at first reading.

Checking presentation Computer software is available that will check the vocabulary, use of words and structure of a document and then flag problems and errors for the user's consideration. Such software has to be based on assumptions about subjects upon which there is no consensus: (a) the correct use of words, and (b) as to what constitutes good English. It should therefore be used as intended: as a guide, not as an obstacle to originality or to the development of one's individual style of writing.

Making more use of your computer

Some who use a computer for word processing, for sending and receiving e-mail, and for finding information, do not appreciate how they can use it in other ways to help them with their writing – with software programs that may already be installed in their computers. For example, a program developed to help users perform a particular task, such as word processing, will probably be installed as part of a suite containing other programs developed to help users with other tasks. You may use these other programs when preparing drawings, diagrams and charts; when preparing pages for desk top publishing; when preparing and delivering presentations; and when preparing and using spreadsheets or databases. And each of these programs may have capabilities that overlap with those of the others.

Desk top publishing

With desk top publishing software, page layouts can be planned in a choice of formats, with tables and figures in appropriate places close to relevant text. The result should be a finished appearance indistinguishable from pages in a printed newsletter, magazine, book or other publication. With improvements in word-processing software, however, the line between word-processing (with a word-processing program) and desk top publishing (with a desk top publishing program) is increasingly difficult to draw, and anyone considering preparing camera ready copy for a publisher should ascertain the publisher's requirements before starting to write.

Preparing presentations

With appropriate software it is easy to prepare: (a) a topic outline for a talk, speaker's notes, visual aids for use during a talk as overhead projector transparencies or as slides (see Figure 1.1 and 4.1), and (b) handouts providing further details, for distribution after a talk. Slides (images stored electronically on a disk) can be prepared with or without a background colour and design; and both visual aids and handouts can include words alone, tables, charts or other artwork, and photographs. However, care should be taken that the choice of background (see also page 91), or the use of special effects, is not such as to distract listeners – who should be concentrating on your message.

In preparing and delivering your talk, remember that it is what you say – supported by any audio-visual aids – that forms your presentation (not your visual aids alone). Speak to your audience. Maintain eye contact as you talk. Do not look at the screen, and do not read aloud for your audience the words on the screen that you have displayed for people to read for themselves.

Do not attempt to say too much. Keep your message simple. Pause when necessary: for example to give everyone time to study each visual aid undisturbed by the sound of your voice, and to allow a few seconds for thought after you make each important point – so that everyone knows you have said what you have to say about it and are about to start talking about something else.

Using spreadsheets

In a spreadsheet, data are entered in a table in which vertical ruled lines between the columns and horizontal ruled lines between the rows form a grid in which the resulting spaces are called cells. Whereas in a printed table, on a page, the number of columns and rows is limited by the type size used and by page size, a spreadsheet can be much larger – according to your needs. You can store data in cells and by entering appropriate formulae in other cells you can perform calculations, analyse numerical data, and obtain statistics, as with a calculator. Furthermore, data saved on a disk can be edited and if you need to change an entry or add data in extra cells, or even add or delete whole columns or rows of data, the calculations are repeated almost immediately and automatically by the computer. You do not have to calculate or recalculate.

Spreadsheets can be used for keeping records of your personal finances, and in business, for example, for recording and analysing sales data, and for accounts. As in word processing, spreadsheets can be printed as hard copy, and if necessary can be incorporated in word-processed documents. Results of the analysis of data, recorded on spreadsheets, can also be used to produce graphs, histograms and charts, and these too can be incorporated in word-processed documents (or in the handouts and visual aids used in presentations).

Preparing and using a database

In a database, which should not be confused with a spreadsheet, data are recorded electronically in a table and stored in a computer instead of in a filing cabinet or card index. Advantages of an electronic database are that: (a) it occupies less space than would a filing cabinet or card index used to store the same information, (b) records can be sorted easily and quickly –

and data extracted – according to one's immediate needs, (c) it is easy to add, correct and delete records to keep them up-to-date, and (e) records are not lost or incorrectly filed – and so unavailable – as a result of the careless-ness of some users.

Anyone with good software skills should be able to design, construct and maintain a simple database, using a desktop PC program, but few stu-dents will need such records (which in business could be used, for example, in keeping up-to-date staff records, or for stock records and stock control).

Looking after your documents

1 Information obtained via the internet, including attachments to incoming e-mail messages, might be contaminated with viruses, and should be checked before opening.

2 Before using a computer, therefore, ensure that it has up-to-date virus-detecting and virus-removing software installed.

3 Before using a disk for the first time, ensure that it is checked for viruses with an up-to-date virus checker.

4 When producing a new document, use a new disk and backup disk for just that document.

5 Save (or file) your work frequently, as you plan, write, correct or revise a document, so that if anything is lost (for example, as a result of a power failure) you do not lose much of the document and can try to do the work again quickly while the information and ideas are still fresh in your mind.

6 Save your work before you try any new commands if there is any possi-bility that you may lose or inadvertently alter part or all of the document, so that you can quit (that is, leave the document in its orig-inal state) and try again.

7 Your floppy disks may go wrong, as may the hard disk of your personal computer, causing you to lose all your work at any time. So ensure that all data stored in a computer are backed up with a frequency that reflects their value and importance. Take a local copy immediately after data have been entered from memory, or from an enquiry or investigation. Each day, when working on a document, make a new copy using a different file name (for example, the year, month and day). If you are working on a document for several days, or for several weeks, take daily, weekly and monthly backups on separate disks. Bear in mind that disks are inexpensive, whereas your time spent in re-entering lost information – if this were possible – would cost much more and would interfere with your other work.

8 Label your disks consecutively (for example, with your initials and a

number: ABC001, ABC002, etc.) and maintain a log of your disks in a small hardback notebook. Record what each disk contains, and for backup disks record the type of backup (daily, weekly, or monthly).

9   When a document is complete, copy it into your master archive disk, and backup archive disk, in case you need copies later, or need to update it or to include parts in another document.

10 Reformat your document disk ready for your next document.

11 Do not carry all your disks with you at one time. Keep your master archive and master backup disks in separate places, so that if one is lost or damaged you still have the other.

12 As well as backing up your files on disk, and keeping your disks in a safe place separate from your computer, you are advised to insure your computer against loss due to accident or theft. This is especially important with a portable computer (which you should never leave unattended).

Looking after yourself when using a computer

1   Sit comfortably at your computer. Adjust your chair so that you are close to the desk, with your elbows level with the computer keyboard, your feet resting flat on the floor or on a foot rest, and your back upright. When using a mouse, rest your arm on the desk and move your hand by moving the elbow rather than the wrist. If you touch type, you could try using a contoured keyboard.

2   Adjust the height of the visual display unit, if necessary, so that your eyes are level with the top of the screen and 30 to 60 cm from the screen.

3   Ensure that the screen is clean and free from glare (for example, from a lamp or window) and that the keyboard and your working surface are sufficiently illuminated – but have a matt surface that does not reflect light.

4   If necessary, adjust the brightness and contrast controls on your visual display unit, so that the background is no brighter than is necessary for you to see the words clearly.

5   If you cannot touch type you will find it tiring to be constantly looking down at the keyboard, and at your handwritten draft, and then up at the screen. But if you can touch type you will not need to look at the keyboard when copy typing and may find it helpful to use a document holder to hold your papers adjacent to the screen.

6   Do not allow the use of a computer to become an end in itself. A computer helps you to do many things, some of which would not otherwise be possible (for example, in recording, processing, storing, and retrieving information); but in study and at work much time can also be

wasted in fruitless activity. When seeking information, try to find just the information you need as quickly as possible. When word processing, take care at all stages in the preparation of a document – but recognise when it will serve its purpose and the job is done.

7 As an aid to concentration, work to a job list (see page 10) and organise your work so that you engage in different activities. In particular, it is not a good idea to sit still – staring at a screen – for long periods. Take a break of at least five minutes every hour, exercising, relaxing or working in a different way. This will help you to concentrate and will reduce fatigue.

Although you may be able to make more use of your computer to help you with your writing, you are advised to organise your work so that you spend no more time than you have to actually sitting and looking at a computer screen.

Purchasing a computer

Anyone considering buying a computer is advised, first, to complete a basic course in computing – leading to an award such as the European Computer Driving Licence (for example the British Computer Society's Certificate in Information Technology which includes the study of the basic concepts of information technology, using a computer and managing files, information and communication, word processing, spreadsheets, databases, presentations and graphics, and using information technology).

Then, if you are considering buying a new personal computer because you are starting a college or university course, you are advised not to buy it until you know (a) what equipment will be available for your use in the institution you will be attending, and (b) what you are expected to provide yourself. When you have actually started the course you will be in a better position to know your hardware and software requirements. Most students in higher education should find that they have open access to a networked desktop computer; and in some institutions, for some courses, they will also either be supplied with or required to buy a laptop (see page 192).

Anyone selecting and purchasing a computer is likely to have conflicting requirements, so some cannot be completely satisfied. Some conflicting requirements result from the increasing rate of technological change. For example on the one hand obsolescence may make it desirable to update software as soon as possible, and on the other hand the costs involved in purchasing new software and in acquiring new skills may make it necessary to delay making such changes.

In relation to both the cost of purchasing a computer system and the decision as to the best time to buy, bear in mind also that any computer or information technology equipment you are thinking of buying will cost less, or will be obsolete and replaced by a more powerful and cheaper system, if you wait. The longer you wait, the better value you may expect to obtain for your money.

Then, when you are ready to buy a computer, check that it includes backup and restore facilities. Obtain proof that the backup/restore method does provide: (a) the ability to backup and restore selected folders/files (as distinct from a whole disk or partition); (b) full backup (recording the backup date against each file); (c) incremental backup (backup of files not already backed-up – since either the last full or the last incremental backup, whichever was last); (d) differential backup (backup of all files changed since the last full backup); and (e) disk spanning (which allows you to backup files that are larger than the capacity of the backup media).

Having acquired backup software, familiarise yourself with it. Ensure that it works both ways (for backing up and for restoring files) and that you can restore the files to at least one other computer, as well as your own.

When buying a desktop computer, choose one that can be fitted with more than one hard disk. Then you will be able to copy all your important data on to another disk. If this disk is removable you can store it in a separate location, away from your computer, for safe keeping: so check that the computer has an access slit for inserting and extracting a removable hard disk. Hard disks are very reliable and are inexpensive (that is to say, their price:data storage ratio is good).

However, you may be asked to buy a portable computer that will satisfy all your requirements as a student – for example, to access your timetables, course materials and library catalogues; to prepare and submit assignments; to communicate with your tutors and with other students via an intranet; and to access the internet. If you are required to buy a computer you should also be given detailed advice as to precisely what hardware and software are needed, and how best they may be obtained.

14 What is the point?

A quick guide to punctuation

Some people suggest that mistakes in grammar (the art of speaking, reading and writing correctly) do not matter in speaking and writing if the meaning intended is clear; but if the English is poor the meaning is unlikely to be clear.

In writing, punctuation marks (*points*: the comma, semicolon, colon, full stop, question mark, exclamation mark, bracket and dash) indicate the pauses that in speech help to make the meaning of a sentence clear. For example, without pauses when speaking or punctuation in writing the meaning of this sentence is not clear:

> This latest outbreak of violence has not surprisingly received the condemnation of politicians of all parties.

To make clear whether or not the rioting has been condemned, in writing commas are needed after surprisingly and *either* before *or* after not.

> This latest outbreak of violence has, not surprisingly, received . . .

> This latest outbreak of violence has not, surprisingly, received . . .

However, it is best to use no more words, and no more punctuation marks (no more points), than are necessary. So, to make the meaning clearer, without punctuation, and without the excruciating adverb surprisingly, it would be better to write, without bias:
either

> This latest outbreak of violence has been condemned by . . .

or

> This latest outbreak of violence has not been condemned by . . .

Using punctuation marks to make your meaning clear

In writing, other marks (see apostrophe, quotation marks, and hyphen, pages 199–201) are used with punctuation marks to help to make a writer's meaning clear. For example:

> The Prime Minister said, 'The Leader of the Opposition is a fool.'

> 'The Prime Minister', said the Leader of the Opposition, 'is a fool.'

The meaning of the first of these sentences is the opposite of that of the second, but the words, and the order of words, are identical.

If you have difficulty with punctuation you will find it easiest to write in short sentences. For example:

> A sentence begins with a capital letter. It includes a verb. It ends with a full stop. It expresses a whole thought, or a few closely connected thoughts. It therefore makes sense by itself.

Each of the last five sentences expresses one thought, telling the reader one thing about a sentence, but if you were to write only in short sentences your reader would have no sooner started reading each one than it would be time to stop. For people who read well, therefore, a whole document written in short sentences would be hard reading – not easy reading.

Using punctuation marks to ensure the smooth flow of language

The thoughts expressed in the five short sentences can be expressed in two.

> A sentence starts with a capital letter, includes a verb, and ends with a full stop. Because it expresses a whole thought or a few closely connected thoughts, it makes sense by itself.

In different sentences you may use the same words to express different thoughts.

> You can help. Can you help?

Conversely, you may use different words to express the same thought.

> Please come here. You come here. Come here, you!

Table 14.1 Parts of speech: classifying words

Parts of speech	The work words do in a sentence*
Verbs	Words used to indicate action: what is done, or what was done, or what is said to be. The ship *sailed*.
Nouns	Names. *Nelson* sailed his ship.
Pronouns	Words used instead of nouns or so that nouns need not be repeated. *He* sailed in *her*.
Adjectives	Words that describe or qualify nouns or pronouns. The *big* ship sailed across the *shallow sea*.
Adverbs	Words that modify verbs, adjectives and other adverbs. The big ship sailed *slowly* across the *gently* rolling sea.
Prepositions	Each preposition governs, and marks the relation between, a noun or pronoun and some other word in the sentence. The ship sailed *across* the sea *to* America.
Conjunctions	Words used to join the parts of a sentence, or to make two sentences into one. The ship went to America *and* came straight back.

Note
* A word may do different work (act as different parts of speech). For example, Phythian (1985) in *Good English* gives: Put it *down* (adverb). Walk *down* the hill (preposition). The pillows are filled with goose *down* (noun). There is a *down* payment (adjective). They decided to *down* tools (verb).

Using conjunctions to contribute to the smooth flow of language

Conjunctions (for example, and, but, for, when, which, because) can be used to join parts of a sentence or to make two sentences into one (see Table 14.1). They link closely related thoughts, give continuity to your writing, and so help your readers along. However, use each conjunction intelligently, and preferably not more than once in a sentence. Remember, also, that some conjunctions must be used in pairs: *both* is always followed by *and*, *either* by *or*, *neither* by *nor*, and *not only* by *but also*.

Using capital letters

In handwriting a clear distinction should be made between capital letters (upper case) and small letters (lower case); and (except possibly in a signature) capitals should not be used as an embellishment.

A capital initial letter is used for the first word of a sentence, interjection or heading, for most words in the titles of publications (see page 209), and for proper nouns (proper names) including trade names (see page 109).

> Our church is St Ann's Church.

A capital initial letter is no longer used to emphasise a word that is not a proper noun (see page 73).

Whole words in chapter headings, and in the section headings of a report, may be written in capitals. Otherwise, capital letters are rarely used for whole words – but acronyms are written in capitals so that they cannot be mistaken for words, for example, WHO (World Health Organization) to distinguish it from the word 'who', unless the acronym has been accepted as a word (as have radar and scuba).

For examples of the use of capital letters in abbreviations and contractions, see page 65.

Punctuation marks that end a sentence

If you find punctuation difficult, begin by mastering the use of the full stop and keep your sentences short: come quickly to the point.

Full stop, question mark and exclamation mark

The end of a sentence or interjection is indicated by a full stop, question mark, or exclamation mark.

> You must go. Ha. Oh. Must you go? Go!

The full stop is also used after an abbreviation (see page 65); and three full stops in a row are used to mark an incomplete sentence (see page 22) and to indicate where words have been omitted in a quotation (see page 18). Titles, awards and acronyms are written without full stops (for example, Dr, BSc, UNESCO).

Remember that a question mark is used only after a direct question.

> Could you explain, please?
>
> I should appreciate an explanation.
>
> I wonder if I should ask for an explanation.
>
> Please explain. Explain!

Exclamation marks are rarely used in scholarly writing; and in business and technical communications they are used only to signpost a warning. Caution! Danger! Stop!

Punctuation marks used within a sentence

The punctuation marks used to separate parts of a sentence make the reader pause for a shorter time than does a full stop. The more you read and write, the more you will come to appreciate their value in helping you to communicate your thoughts precisely.

Comma

Items in a list may be separated by commas, as they are in the next sen tence. To write clear, concise and easily read prose we use commas, semicolons, colons, dashes, and brackets. In such a list the comma before the final *and* is essential only if it contributes to clarity.

A comma may also be used to separate the parts (or clauses) in a sentence. The word clause comes from the Latin word *claudere*, to close, and within a sentence commas may be needed to separate (close off) one thought or statement from the next.

A sentence comprising one clause, expressing only one thought, is called a simple sentence. It makes one statement.

Each word should contribute to the sentence.

Each sentence should contribute to the paragraph.

Each paragraph should contribute to the composition.

Nothing should be superfluous.

However, a sentence may comprise more than one clause – expressing more than one thought. A comma or a conjunction, or both, may then be inserted between the separate statements (clauses):

Each word should contribute to the sentence, each sentence to the paragraph, and each paragraph to the composition. Nothing should be superfluous.

Note that in this example, at the beginning of the second clause the conjunction (and) is understood: there is no need to write it. Similarly, in each clause there is a verb but in the second and third clauses this verb (contribute) is understood.

Use commas to mark separate clauses if they make for easy reading and help you to convey your thoughts. A commenting clause should be enclosed by commas; a defining clause should not be.

Nurses, who work on Sundays, are . . .

Nurses who work on Sundays are . . .

Note the difference in meaning. The first sentence implies that all nurses work on Sundays. The second sentence identifies or defines which nurses are referred to: those who do work on Sundays.

A comma is used either after, or before and after, some linking adverbs (conjunctive adverbs), for emphasis, usually at or near the beginning of a sentence. For example:

Furthermore, . . .	There are, also, . . .
However, this is also true of . . .	There are, however, many . . .
Moreover, . . . Also, . . .	We observed, moreover, that . . .
Otherwise, . . .	It is possible, nevertheless, to see . . .
Therefore, . . .	Note, therefore, that . . .

Other conjunctive adverbs include: accordingly, again, besides, consequently, for, hence, incidentally, indeed, instead, likewise, namely, so, still, then, thus, yet.

Do not add commas at random because you feel that a sentence is too long to be without punctuation marks. Either put the comma in the right place, to convey your meaning, or write the sentence so that your meaning is conveyed clearly without the comma. For example:

You will be informed, if you send a stamped addressed envelope, after the meeting.

You will be informed, if you send a stamped addressed envelope after the meeting.

If you send a stamped addressed envelope you will be informed after the meeting.

Note that the first and third sentences convey the same message; one with commas and the other without.

Brackets and dashes

Brackets (whether curved or square) are used in pairs (to bracket, enclose), and dashes may be used in pairs – as here – when an aside (a parenthesis) is added to a sentence. So if you removed the asides from the last sentence you would be left with a complete sentence. Each aside is said to be in parenthesis.

Use curved brackets (which some people call parentheses) when you wish to insert a cross-reference (see page 14), an example (see page 32), or an explanation (as in the first sentence of this section).

Use dashes to give prominence to an insertion (as in the next paragraph). But note that commas could be used instead of dashes, as in this sentence, if you wished to give less prominence to an aside. One dash can be used if an aside is added at the end of a sentence – as in this sentence. Use square brackets when you insert your own words into a quotation (see page 2).

Note that one space should be left before the opening bracket and one space after the closing bracket; but that – to distinguish it from a hyphen – a space is left both before and after a dash.

Colon and semicolon

A colon may be used to introduce a list (as on page 2) or a quotation (as on page 29); and may also be used, in place of a full stop, either (a) between two statements of equal weight (as on page 35) or (b) between two statements if the second is an explanation or elaboration of the first (as on page 43).

The full stop (or period), question mark, exclamation mark, colon, semicolon, dash, comma, and bracket are all punctuation marks, points or stops. They all indicate pauses. The full stop gives the longest and most impressive pause. The colon gives a shorter pause. Use of the semicolon, which gives a shorter pause than a colon but a longer pause than a comma, may contribute to clarity (for examples, see pages 12, 13, and 14).

Other essential marks

Apostrophe

The apostrophe is the mark that causes the greatest or most obvious difficulty for many who have been taught English in British schools. If you are not sure about its use, first note that an apostrophe is *never* used in forming the plural: apple becomes apples; criterion, criteria; datum, data; gateau, gateaux; lady, ladies; man, men; mouse, mice; phenomenon, phenomena; and wife, wives. Then note that if, in scholarly writing, you avoid collo-quial language (see page 71), in which an apostrophe is used to mark a contraction (for example, can't *for* cannot, don't *for* do not, it's *for* it is or it has, that's *for* that is, there's *for* there is, they're *for* they are, who's *for* who is, and won't *for* will not), you will use an apostrophe only when you wish to indicate that someone or something belongs to someone or something (see pages 203–4).

An *s* is added to many nouns (names of things, see Table 14.1) to make them plural: book becomes books; but man becomes men. To indicate own-ership either an apostrophe s ('s) is added to a word (book's and men's) or just an apostrophe is added (books'). For example: the cat's dinner (the dinner of the cat); the cats' dinner (the dinner of the cats); the man's books (the books belonging to the man); the men's books (the books belonging to the men); the books' covers (the covers of the books); the book's cover (the cover of the book). So the distinction in English between the cat's dinner and the cats' dinner is grammatical, even though for anyone learn-ing the language it may at first be a difficulty in spelling.

Write Dr Smith's office (for the office of Dr Smith) but, because the name ends in an s, it is easier to say Dr Jones' office than Dr Jones's office and both are acceptable (for the office of Dr Jones).

Note that 1990's music (apostrophe before the *s*) is the music of 1990, and 1990s' music (apostrophe after the *s*) is the music of the 1990s (the ten years from 1990 to 1999), no apostrophe being required when simply forming the plural.

Do not add an apostrophe and *s*, to indicate ownership, to a word that in itself indicates ownership (a possessive adjective or a possessive pronoun – see list on page 204). However, note that the words one, -one and body, when used as possessive pronouns, do require an apostrophe (as in one's, someone's, everyone's, nobody's, somebody's and everybody's).

Hyphen

The hyphen is a mark used in forming two words into one: for example, in ordinal and cardinal numbers (see page 86), in boat-house for a building in which boats are housed, and house-boat for a boat used as a house.

As a new word formed in this way becomes established in the language the hyphen may be omitted. Potter (1966) gives these examples: no body (14th to 18th centuries), no-body (17th and 18th centuries, and nobody (since the eighteenth century); and the two words book and mark, joined at first as book-mark but now written bookmark.

The hyphen is also used: (a) to distinguish, for example, between recount (to give an account of) and re-count (to count again), and between relay (to send a message) and re-lay (to lay again as in re-laying a cable); (b) in some words after the prefixes anti, inter, neo, non, over, sub and under (for example, anti-bacterial but antiseptic, non-existent but nonconformist, neo-Latin but neologism, sub-standard but submarine); (c) in some titles (for example, vice-principal); (d) in some words to separate identical letters (for example, book-keeping, mis-spell and pre-eminent) to make for easy reading.

Another use of the hyphen, in books, is to join two syllables when a word is broken at the end of a line of print. But in handwriting it is not necessary to break words between lines; and in word processing it is not usual to justify the right-hand margin – so it is rarely necessary to use hyphens at the ends of lines. Note that a space is left both before and after the dash in the last sentence; but no space is left either before or after a hyphen.

Quotation marks

You may use quotation marks (inverted commas) when you quote someone else's words exactly (as on pages 17 and 29), or you may signpost extracts by headings (see Table 6.1 and pages 82–3) or by indentation in the text and an acknowledgement (as on page 3) – including quotation marks only if they are part of the extract (as on pages 76–7).

When quoting someone else's work, the part quoted must be complete – including every word and every punctuation mark. Any gaps in the quotation should be indicated (by three dots, preceded and followed by a space, as on page 3) and any words you insert in a quotation (for clarification, further explanation, or to summarise) must be in square brackets (as on page 6). The source of each quotation should normally be acknowledged (see page 3), unless you have some good reason for not doing so (for example, see page xiv).

Do not use quotation marks (inverted commas) to indicate that a word or phrase is not to be understood in its usual sense, because if you do the intended sense may not be clear to the reader. Instead, choose words that convey your meaning precisely (see page 54).

The titles of books, plays and poems should not be marked by quotation marks, as is sometimes recommended, but in handwriting by underlining and in print by italics (or underlining).Use underlining or italics to help you distinguish, for example, between David Copperfield (the name of a character in a book) and *David Copperfield* (the title of a book).

Improve your writing

The best way to appreciate the usefulness of different punctuation marks is to study one or two pages of any book or article that interests you. Consider why the author has used each punctuation mark. You can repeat this exercise with as many compositions as you choose to study. In writing clear and simple English you can manage without semicolons and colons, but as you begin to appreciate their value you will want to use them.

Your writing, including your punctuation and spelling, will also improve – without your making any conscious effort to improve it – if you read well-written books and newspapers regularly for enlightenment and pleasure.

15 Spelling check

Mistakes in spelling, as with mistakes in punctuation and grammar, reduce an educated reader's confidence in a writer. They also distract readers, taking their attention away from the writer's message. Spelling correctly, therefore, is part of efficient communication.

Some reasons for poor spelling

Some words are not spelt as they are pronounced. For example, answer (anser), gauge (gage), island (iland), mortgage (morgage), psychology (sycology), rough (ruff), sugar (shugar) and tongue (tung). You cannot, therefore, spell all words as you pronounce them. This is one problem for people who find spelling difficult.

However, those who speak badly are likely to find that incorrect pronunciation does lead to incorrect spelling. In lazy speech secretary becomes secatray; environment, enviroment; police, pleece; computer, compu'er; and so on. If you know that you speak and spell badly, take more care over your speech.

Unfortunately, the speech of teachers and that of announcers on radio and television does not necessarily provide a reliable guide to pronunciation. Consult a dictionary, therefore, if you are unsure of the pronunciation or spelling of a word. And, when you consult a dictionary to see how a word is spelt, check the pronunciation at the same time. Knowing how to pronounce the word correctly, you may have no further difficulty in spelling it correctly.

Many people have difficulty in spelling some words correctly because they are unable to distinguish between there and their, its and it's, whose and who's, book and book's, books and books'.

If you cannot decide which to use, avoid colloquial language (see page 71) and learn how to indicate ownership.

Their and theirs are used to indicate that something belongs to some people or to some thing. Remember this rule: *e* in her, *i* in his, *e* and *i* in their and theirs, to indicate possession.

There is used with the verb to be. Remember: there is, there are, there was, there were *t h e r e* spells there. This spelling is also used for a place:

Is anyone there? There is their house, over there.

My, his, her, its, our, your and their are possessive adjectives: my book, her eyes, its leaves, and their house. Mine, his, hers, its, ours, yours and theirs are possessive pronouns:

This book is mine; this is yours, and these are theirs.

To distinguish its (possessive) from it's (colloquial: a contraction), remember that it's means *either* it is *or* it has. It's has no other meaning. See also *Apostrophe*, page 199. Remember, also, that colloquial language should not be used in scholarly writing or business communications (except when reporting conversation – in quotation marks). Instead, use standard English or standard American (see page 71).

Some rules to remember

The best way to improve your spelling is to consult a dictionary and then to memorise the correct spelling of any word that you find you have spelt incorrectly. However, learning the following rules – one at a time – will also help.

1 When *ie* or *ei* are pronounced *ee*, the *i* comes before the *e* except after *c* (as in believe and receive). Exceptions to this rule are seize and species. In eight, either, foreign, freight, reign, their, weight and weir the *ei* is not pronounced *ee*, so the *i* does not come before the *e*.

2 When words ending in *fer* are made longer (for example when refer is used in making the longer words reference and referred) the *r* is not doubled if, in pronouncing the longer word, you stress the first syllable (as in *re*ference), but it is doubled if you stress the second syllable (as in re*fer*red). A syllable is a unit of pronunciation which forms a word or a part of a word.

	First stress	*Second stress*
defer	*defer*ence	de*fer*red, de*fer*ring
differ	*differ*ence, *differ*ing	

infer	*inf*erence	in*fer*red, in*fer*ring
offer	*off*ered, *off*ering	
refer	*ref*eree, *ref*erence	re*fer*red, re*fer*ring
suffer	*suff*ering, *suff*erance	
transfer	*trans*ference	trans*fer*red, trans*fer*ring

3 With verbs of more than one syllable that end with a single vowel (*a, e, i, o* or *u*) followed by a single consonant (a letter that is not a vowel), in forming the past tense or a present or past participle double the consonant if the last syllable is stressed.

	First stress	*Second stress*
benefit	*bene*fited, *bene*fiting	
bias	*bi*ased	
control		con*trol*led, con*trol*ling
excel		ex*cel*led, ex*cel*ling
focus	*fo*cused, *fo*cusing	
parallel	*par*alleled	
refer		re*fer*red, re*fer*ring

There are exceptions to this rule, including funnel (funnelled), model (modelled), panel (panelled), rival (rivalled), travel (travelled) and tunnel (tunnelled).

4 With verbs of one syllable that end with a single vowel followed by a single consonant, double the consonant before adding ing.

run	running
sag	sagging
swim	swimming
whip	whipping

But if a verb of one syllable does not end in a single vowel followed by a single consonant, simply add ing.

daub	daubing
deal	dealing
feel	feeling
help	helping
sink	sinking
watch	watching

5 When verbs ending in e are made into words ending in ing the e is lost.

bite	biting
come	coming
make	making
trouble	troubling
write	writing

But there are exceptions:

agree	agreeing (to keep the ee sound)
dye	dyeing (colouring)
flee	fleeing (to keep the ee sound)
hoe	hoeing
singe	singeing (to keep the soft g)

And with some verbs the ie ending is replaced by y:

die	dying
lie	lying

6 If an adjective ends in l, the corresponding adverb (which answers the question How?) ends in lly.

beautiful	beautifully
faithful	faithfully
hopeful	hopefully
peaceful	peacefully
spiteful	spitefully

7 Some adjectives that end in y have corresponding adverbs and nouns in which the y is replaced by an i.

busy	busily	business
merry	merrily	merriment

Improve your writing

Read good prose

If you do not read very much, you give yourself few opportunities to see words spelt correctly and to increase your vocabulary. Reading good prose will help you in these and other ways (see *Read good English*, page 109).

Spelling test

Ask someone to test your spelling of these words:

absence, accelerate, accessible, accidentally, accommodation*,
achieve, acquaint, address, advertisement, altogether, analogous,
ancillary, apparent, attendance, audience, auxiliary,
beautiful, beginning, benefited, bureaucracy, business*
calendar, census, cereal, certain, competence, conscience,
conscientious, conscious, consensus, commitment, committee,
correspondence, criticism,
decision, definite, desiccated, desperate, develop, disappear,
disappointed,
embarrass, environment, eradicate, especially, exaggerate,
existence,
faithfully, fascinate, February, forty, fourth, fulfil, fulfilled,
gauge, government, grammar, grateful, guarantee,
harassment, harmful, height*, hierarchy, humorous,
idiosyncrasy, incidentally, independent, irradiate,
liaison, library, loose, lose, lying
maintenance, management, misspell, millennium, minuscule,
minutes
necessary*, noticeably,
occasion, occurrence, omit, omitted,
parallel, parliament, personnel, planning, possess, precede,
privilege, procedure, proceed, profession, pronunciation,
publicly, pursued,
quiet, quite,
receipt, receive, recommend, relevant, restaurant, rhythm,
scissors, secretary, seize, separate*, severely, siege, sincerely*,
successful, supersede, surprising, syllable,
unnecessarily, until,
Wednesday, wholly,
yield.

Note: In a survey of 1000 adults for the Adult Literacy and Basic Skills Unit (*The Guardian*, 12 November 1992), only 166 spelt all six of the words marked with an asterisk in this list correctly, and 730 spelt accommodation incorrectly.

Take an interest in etymology: the study of the origins of words

Knowing the origin of a word (see *Dictionaries*, page 116) may help you to understand its spelling. For example, the word separate is derived from a Latin word *separare* (to separate or divide); so is the word pare (to cut, for example one's nails, or to peel, for example potatoes); but desperate, from the Latin *sperare* (to hope), means without hope.

Keep a good dictionary on your bookshelf

Always have a good dictionary (see page 209) available for reference when you are thinking, reading or writing. Do not get into the habit of using another word when you are unsure of the spelling of the most appropriate word. Instead, always refer to a dictionary so that you can use the word that best conveys your meaning. Make a note, from your dictionary, of the correct spelling of any words you spell incorrectly (as indicated, for example, by a spell checker on your computer) so that you can memorise the correct spelling.

References

Dictionaries

A good dictionary gives the spelling, punctuation and meaning of each word, its use in current English (for example, n = noun, colloq = colloquial, sl = slang), its derivatives (words formed from it), and its derivation (origins). Make sure that your dictionary gives all this information, and keep it to hand, for ready reference, on your bookshelf.

Suitable dictionaries for students include Chambers' *Twentieth Century Dictionary* (Edinburgh, Chambers), *Collins English Dictionary* (London, Collins), the *Concise Oxford English Dictionary* (Oxford, Oxford University Press) and *Webster's Dictionary of English Usage* (Mass., Merriam-Webster).

Further reading

Most of the publications listed here are referred to in the text. Notes after the bibliographic details of some works are to help readers appreciate their usefulness.

Barrass, R. (2001) *Study! A Guide to Effective Learning, Revision and Examination Techniques*, 2nd edition, London: Routledge.

Barrass, R. (2002) *Writing at Work: A Guide to Better Writing in Administration, Business and Management*, London: Routledge.

Bullock, A. (1975) *A Language for Life*, London: HMSO. Includes a forthright note of dissent by Stuart Froome, concerning the relationship between declining standards in the use of English by pupils and changes in teaching methods in the 1960s.

Butler, S. (1903) *Ernest Pontifax or The Way of All Flesh*, 1965 edition. D. F. Howard, ed., London: Methuen.

Dearing, R. (1997) *Higher Education in the Learning Society: Report of the National Committee of Inquiry into Higher Education*, London: HMSO.

Evans, H. (1972) *Editing and Design: Book 1 Newsman's English*, London: Heinemann (page 206).

Flesch, R. F. (1962) *The Art of Plain Talk*, London and New York: Collier-Macmillan. Includes advice on writing as well as on speaking.

Fowler, H. W. (1968) *A Dictionary of Modern English Usage*, 2nd edition rev. E. Gowers, Oxford: Clarendon Press.

Fowler, H. W. and Fowler, F. G. (1906) *The King's English*, Oxford: Clarendon Press.

Gash, S. (1989) *Effective Literature Searching for Students*, Aldershot: Gower.

Gowers, E. (1986) *The Complete Plain Words*, 3rd edition rev. S. Greenbaum and J. Whitcut, London: HMSO.

Graves, R. and Hodge, A. (1947) *The Reader Over Your Shoulder: A Handbook for Writers of English Prose*, 2nd edition, London: Cape; New York: Macmillan.

Jay, A. (1933) *Effective Presentations*, London: Pitman (for Institute of Management).

Johnson, S. (1759) *The History of Rasselas: Prince of Abyssinia*, London: Folio Society.

Kingman, J. (1988) *Report of the Committee of Inquiry into the Teaching of English Language*, Department of Education and Science, London: HMSO. In which one member of the committee, Professor H. G. Widdowson, expresses his regrets that the committee does not clearly define English as a subject. See also Sampson (1925) in this list.

McCartney, E. S. (1953) *Recurrent Maladies in Scholarly Writing*, Ann Arbor: University of Michigan Press.

Maugham, W. S. (1938) *The Summing Up*, London: Heinemann.

Mullen, J. (1997) Graduates deficient in 'soft' skills, *People Management*, 3 (22) 18.

Napley, D. (1975) *The Technique of Persuasion*, 2nd edition, London: Sweet and Maxwell.

Newbolt, H. (1921) *The Teaching of English in England*, London: HMSO.

Orwell, G. (1946) Politics and the English Language, *Horizon* No. 76 (April 1946). Reprinted (1957) in *Selected Essays*, Harmondsworth: Penguin Books.

Partridge, E. (1949) *English: A Course for Human Beings*, London, Winchester, page 112.

Partridge, E. (1965) *Usage and Abusage: A Guide to Good English*, 8th edition, London, Hamish Hamilton; New York, British Book Centre.

Perrin, P. G. (1965) *Writer's Guide and Index to English*, 4th edition rev. K. W. Dickens and W. R. Ebbitt, Fair lawn: N.J., Scott, Foresman and Co.

Phythian, B. A. (1985) *Good English*, London: Hodder and Stoughton. A concise, clearly explained introduction to the English language.

Potter, S. (1966) *Our Language*, 2nd edition, Harmondsworth: Penguin Books. *A Concise Introduction to the Origins of English Words, to Their Use, to the Development of English as an International Language, and to Sources of Further Information.*

Quiller-Couch, A. (1916) *On the Art of Writing*, Cambridge: Cambridge University Press.

Sampson, George (1925) *English for the English*, Cambridge: Cambridge University Press. Considers the impact of the Education Act of 1870, over fifty years, asserts the importance of teaching English to the English, and defines precisely what he considers should be the aim and content of the study of English.

Sayers, D. L. (1948) *The Lost Tools of Learning*, London: Methuen, 30 pages.

Strunk, W. and White, E. B. (1999) *The Elements of Style*, 4th edition, Boston: Allyn and Bacon

Tichy, H. J. and Fourdrinier, S. (1988) *Effective Writing for Engineers, Managers, Scientists*, 2nd edition, New York and Chichester: Wiley.

Vallins, G. H. (1964) *Good English: How to Write It*, London and Washington: André Deutsch and Academic Press.

Wojtas, O. (1981) Students who just carnt spel, *Times Higher Education Supplement*, 11 December 1981. Report of a Glasgow University inter-faculty committee's conclusion that fifty percent of English language and literature students needed help with basic writing skills.

Index

Note that, in addition to the words in this index, some pairs of words that many people confuse are listed alphabetically on pages 54–7 (see also page 67); and some other words that many misuse are listed alphabetically on pages 58–60.